D0084770

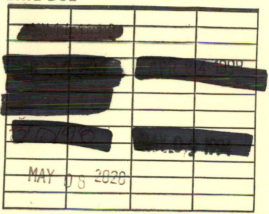

GARRICK CLAIMS THE STAGE

Garrick, an unfinished oil painting by Johann Zoffany. Courtesy E T Archive/Garrick Club.

GARRICK CLAIMS
THE STAGE

Acting as Social
Emblem in
Eighteenth-Century
England

LEIGH WOODS

CONTRIBUTIONS IN DRAMA AND
THEATRE STUDIES, NUMBER 10

GREENWOOD PRESS
Westport, Connecticut
London, England

Library of Congress Cataloging in Publication Data

Woods, Leigh.
  Garrick claims the stage.

  (Contributions in drama and theatre studies,
ISSN 0163-3821 ; no. 10)
    Bibliography: p.
    Includes index.
    1. Garrick, David, 1717–1779.   2. Acting—History—
18th century.   3. Actors—Great Britain—Biography.
4. Theater and society—England.   5. Theater—England—
History—18th century.   I. Title.   II. Series.
PN2598.G3W6   1984   792'.028'0924 [B]   83-18503
ISBN 0-313-24259-3 (lib. bdg.)

Library of Congress Catalog Card Number: 83-18503
ISBN: 0-313-24259-3
ISSN: 0163-3821

First published in 1984

Greenwood Press
A division of Congressional Information Service, Inc.
88 Post Road West
Westport, Connecticut 06881

Printed in the United States of America

10 9 8 7 6 5 4 3 2 1

Copyright Acknowledgment

Grateful acknowledgment is given for the use of excerpts reprinted by permission of the publishers from *The Letters of David Garrick*, ed. by David M. Little
and George M. Kahrl, Cambridge, Mass.: The Belknap Press of Harvard
University Press, Copyright © 1963 by the President and Fellows of Harvard
College.

To Daniel Seltzer
    teacher
    scholar
    actor
    friend

Contents

Illustrations

Acknowledgments

My thanks go to a number of people who saw the manuscript and offered helpful comments on it in various of its stages: to Marc Roth, chairman of my dissertation committee at the University of California, Berkeley; to the other members of the committee, Marvin Rosenberg, William I. Oliver, and David Littlejohn, who responded warmly to my ideas when they were very fresh and tender; to Travis Bogard and Dunbar H. Ogden, also of the University of California, Berkeley; to Dana Sue McDermott, University of California, Riverside; to William Grange, Florida Southern College; and to Marvin Carlson, Indiana University. I am grateful, too, to the Office of Research and Graduate Development at Indiana University for its financial support, and finally, to Joseph Donohue, series editor of the "Contributions in Drama and Theatre Studies" series of Greenwood Press, whose advice and encouragement helped bring the work on this book to its conclusion.

GARRICK CLAIMS THE STAGE

Introduction

Whenever an actor is adopted by a culture, that actor can fairly be said to represent certain composite features of the audience which applauds his efforts on the stage. In the remarkable degree that David Garrick was adopted by the mid-eighteenth-century English theater audience, the resonance between his acting and that which his society found provocative must have been unusual in both its richness and its intensity. This study will attempt to describe the sympathy which existed between Garrick and his public, and it will seek the consistencies between his public functions as an actor—documented and validated as they were by his contemporaries—and his private experience.

This approach departs from the most recent treatments of the actor in the persistence of its attempt to synthesize Garrick's public self with his private one. George Winchester Stone, Jr., and George M. Kahrl's *David Garrick: A Critical Biography* (1979) is the most comprehensive and authoritative of these treatments, as well as the fruit of two distinguished scholarly careers with Garrick at their centers. Although Stone and Kahrl are occasionally critical of eighteenth-century society and its institutions, they shrink from criticizing Garrick himself, and seem to believe the great actor somehow represented the best features of his age without being associated with its worst ones.

Furthermore, owing perhaps to its dual authorship, the book

maintains an essential structural distinction between Garrick's work for the stage and his experience as a private citizen. This distinction seems to me to obscure the dynamic nature of Garrick's achievement as an actor; and it is my belief that his success on the stage lay largely in the extent to which his private concerns bodied forth in his acting, and to which these stood for values either assumed or subscribed to by the great majority of Garrick's audience.

Among other recent treatments of Garrick, the entry on the actor in Volume 6 of Philip H. Highfill, Jr., Kalman A. Burnim, and Edward A. Langhans' *A Biographical Dictionary of Actors . . . in London* (1978) offers a shorter and more dispassionate view of Garrick than do Stone and Kahrl. Its choice of salient events, particularly from Garrick's early life, accords with my own in several cases, although the interpretations which attach to these events in the *Biographical Dictionary* are more narrowly biographical than are those contained in this study. Allardyce Nicoll's *The Garrick Stage* (1980) was completed by Sybil Rosenfeld after Nicoll's death. It treats Garrick as an emblem of his time—as does this book—but its major interest lies not in Garrick himself but in the technical and scenic advances made during the period in which he held the stage, many of which he helped to implement.

There are two organizing principles at work in my examination of Garrick: first, the actor's own personality; and second, the vocabulary used to describe it, and the overlap of that vocabulary into descriptions of his acting. I treat the actor's personality in a thematic way, rather than in a chronological or developmental one. Problems of image-making obsessed Garrick from the time of his childhood, and I explore the particular manifestations of his curious self-consciousness in his work for the stage. The second thread involves the ways in which the terms *sentiment, sympathy*, and *sensibility* were used in Garrick's time in broad and interrelated fashion. All of these words have received extensive treatment in literary and intellectual histories of the period, but I try to demonstrate their pervasiveness as cultural markings through the more pictographic examples offered by Garrick's acting.

The first two chapters of what follows seek to describe the

larger contours of Garrick's life by overlaying images of the popular and intellectual culture of his time with glimpses of him at his work on the stage. The third chapter offers a quick sketch of his roles, examined through the perspective of esthetic and behavioral models which Garrick and his audience seem to have held in common. Chapters 4 and 5 explore conspicuous and re-curring features of Garrick's life away from the stage and their manifestations on the stage. The final chapter seeks to set Gar-rick's career in the context of its moment in British social his-tory. Several of the discussions contained in these chapters try to acknowledge harsher comments about Garrick, as well as to credit the many tributes he received, both as an actor and as a private citizen. Together, the praise and criticism Garrick gath-ered evoke the actor's characteristic ways of responding to stress, and it is not surprising that a distinctive theatricality emerged from his offstage reactions to adversity, at the times he had to face it.

The language of "melting," explored at some length in chap-ter 2, might also have offered the model for the other chapters, each one of which mixes social history with biographical data, criticism, eyewitness accounts, and performance statistics. Par-ticular images of Garrick at his acting are always joined, even-tually, to hypotheses about the society which sanctioned him and his work on the stage. I hope that these juxtapositions between solitary and communal experience, and between public and private frameworks, will begin to supplant the polar images they comprise, and that readers will feel increasingly free to move toward their own images of the intersection between Garrick and his world—and that between the actor and the man—which the facts of his life suggest.

A great and popular actor such as Garrick functions to unify and embody his culture in ways that to some extent transcend the ordinary divisions enforced by social class or by narrow professional interest. Indeed, the definition of any actor's pop-ularity lies precisely in an ability to appeal to people of all kinds, and at all times. This study generalizes a good deal about tend-encies and beliefs which seem to have figured prominently in eighteenth-century English life, but it is the public and consen-sual nature of Garrick's role in the life of his times that prompts such generalizing. His career presents a model for exploring tensions and contradictions central to his age, and the last chapter, in particular, investigates the sense in which the man was himself both a composite and a walking paradox.

Let me point the reader now to Oliver Goldsmith and the beginning of his ironic tribute to his friend,

"Here lies David Garrick, describe me who can . . . "

Goldsmith could, and he did, and so shall we try.

1

The Sources of Dramatic Action on Garrick's Stage

Philosophy in the eighteenth century was characterized by its tendency to challenge and adapt traditional methods of analysis so as to bring them into conformity with the empirical and humanitarian leanings of the age. This tendency was also at work in the widespread questioning of neoclassical esthetics. John Locke's writings, together with the sentimental movement begun by Lord Shaftesbury, were instrumental in precipitating a breakdown of normative esthetic standards and introducing a strain of relativism into broader areas of philosophical inquiry: To what degree is man a free and independent agent, particularly if he is believed to be the product of his continually changing exposure to the material world? To what extent is he able, by his actions, to influence the information which reaches his senses, or the way in which that information affects him once he has received it? To what limits is he able to influence the world around him, rather than merely being influenced by it?

Garrick was an actor and not a philosopher, but by the time of his debut in 1741 there had arisen in England a group of artists who were seeking after an esthetic which could test the ironclad authority which neoclassicism had claimed—and particularly its increasingly uncongenial image of men and women of distinction existing in realms removed from the mundane and creaturely aspects of life. English philosophy of the mid-eighteenth century, in a sort of lockstep with Garrick's acting, would

Garrick Reciting the Ode at the Shakespeare Jubilee. Crown Copyright Victoria and Albert Museum (Theatre Museum).

synthesize an image of man as the creature of minute social obligation, vulnerable to even the most momentary changes in his environment, but as one who commanded some of the older capacity for resolute action. In the title of his work *An Essay on the Nature and Conduct of the Passions*—which Garrick is known to have had in his hands in 1745[1]—Francis Hutcheson indicated his belief that the passions could be managed, together with any actions which such passions might dictate.[2] Persons who believed as Hutcheson did must have undertaken challenges in their lives in the greatest confidence that they themselves held the power to influence the outcome of their actions. As we shall see, it was Garrick's fundamental belief in the efficacy of action and personal initiative, together with the sorts of action he deemed worthy of representation on the stage, which became the most important features of his acting.

As citizen, as businessman, and as artist, Garrick seems not to have experienced the alienation which began to plague artists with the advent of Romanticism. His profession and his natural garrulity exposed him to a variety of behaviors, and they sustained him in an immediate, constant, and diverse contact with

much of the important cultural activity of his day. This familiarity with what amounted to his public seems to have spurred
him continually to refine, expand, and adapt his communica-
tive resources as an actor. In this sense, Garrick was emblematic
of a breed of artists not inclined toward the later Romantic
comparisons between sacred art and gainful, and therefore cor-
rupting and onerous, employment. He manifested neither self-
consciousness nor conspicuous pride at the sudden recognition
of himself as an artist which followed in the wake of his resounding early successes. Indeed, he almost never referred to
himself directly as an artist, and only occasionally invoked the
"genius" which he came to believe in as separating the great actor from the merely technically accomplished one.[3] In his own
mind and in those of his contemporaries, Garrick's reputation
as a man of letters, a man of affairs, and a man of society gave
respectability to the area of his activity about which, to judge it
from his correspondence, he spoke the least, and then almost
always in the most prosaic of terms.

THE PRACTICAL ACTOR

Were we to generalize, then, on the basis of his letters, his
plays, his *An Essay on Acting* (1744), and his passing remarks on
the subject, we would almost certainly conclude that Garrick at
the beginning of his career considered his "art" as an almost
purely practical endeavor. Around the time of his formal debut
on the London stage, as Richard III on October 19, 1741, Garrick wrote to his brother in an attempt to justify his shift from
the wine business which they shared to acting. His improved financial expectations seem to have represented the cutting edge
of his rationale: ". . . as I shall make very near £300 p Annum
by It & as it is what I doat upon I am resolv'd to pursue it";
and he also mentioned the £300 figure in a letter to his cousin,
Peter Fermignac, written at about the same time.[4] In his *Essay*,
Garrick manifested another variety of practicality in laying confident claim to his own objectivity as a critic, proclaiming that
his purposes in writing the piece "are merely Scientifical and
not Subservient to Pique and Partial Prejudice."[5] He also offered a straightforward definition of acting which proclaims its

authority and comprehensiveness by its very phrasing: "Acting is an Entertainment of the Stage, which by calling in the Aid and Assistance of Articulation, Corporeal Motion, and Occular Expression, imitates, assumes, or puts on the various mental and bodily Emotions arising from the various Humours, Virtues, and Vices incident to human Nature."[6] Garrick's tone suggests his belief that acting is readily apprehensible to a general audience. His actual definition of acting requires only one sentence, and the remainder of the approximately thirty-page pamphlet is devoted to the practical demonstration of his theory, lingering not at all on matters theoretical or abstract. His mention of "bodily Emotions" also suggests the degree to which physicality was inherent in his understanding of the "feelings," and of the ways in which sentiment might find expression on the stage.

Garrick continued to explore channels for physical expression in the detailed discussions of his playing of Abel Drugger in Ben Jonson's *The Alchemist* and of Macbeth, which follow in his *Essay*. Garrick moves quickly in each instance from theoretical discussions of the characters' "feelings" to firm technical pronouncements as to how key moments might be rendered by the actor:

When Abel Drugger has broke the Urinal, he is mentally absorb'd with the different Ideas of the invaluable Price of the Urinal, and the Punishment that may be inflicted in Consequence of a Curiosity, no way appertaining or belonging to the Business he came about. Now, if this, as it certainly is, [is] the Situation of his Mind, how are the different members of the Body to be agitated? Why Thus—His Eyes must be revers'd from the Object he is most intimidated with, and by dropping his Lip at the some [*sic*] Time to the Object, it throws a trembling Languour upon every Muscle, and by declining the right Part of the Head towards the Urinal, it casts the most comic Terror and Shame over all the upper Part of the Body, that can be imagin'd. . . .

Now to Macbeth. —When the Murder of Duncan is committed, from an immediate Consciousness of the Fact, his Ambition is ingulph'd at that Instant, by the Horror of the Deed; his faculties are intensely rivited [*sic*] to the Murder alone, without having the least Consolation of the consequential Advantages, to comfort him in the Exigency. He should at that Time, be a moving Statue, or indeed a petrify'd Man;

his Eyes must Speak, and Tongue be metaphorically Silent: his Ears must be sensible of imaginary Noises, and deaf to the present and audible Voice of his Wife; his Attitudes must be quick and permanent; his Voice articulately trembling, and confusedly intelligible. . . . [7]

In each description, Garrick sketches the character's situation and "feeling" in bold strokes, and he then moves quickly to the bodily adjustments for which that situation and sentiment call. These bodily adjustments, in turn, are ones which incorporate elements of tension, confusion, and ambivalence in the characters—in Abel's comic reluctance to look at the broken urinal, even as his lower lip is being drawn toward it, or in Macbeth's voice "articulately trembling, and confusedly intelligible." Such conflicting elements in the characters' behavior lend subtlety to their moments of stress—and "action," in its kinesthetic sense, is given a charged and dynamic quality by each character's reluctance either to undertake bold action or to acknowledge the true depths of his feeling.

With such "practical" physical choices, Garrick began to modify the older, broader style of heroic acting with a more sophisticated psychological awareness. Such awareness, we are to gather, was nowhere evident in the acting of James Quin, Garrick's great rival in the early years of his career and the upholder of heroic acting in the playing of Macbeth, in particular. As Garrick satirized Quin's performance, " 'Come let me clutch thee' is not to be done by one Motion only, but by several successive Catches at it, first with one Hand, and then with the other, preserving the same Motion at the same Time, with his Feet." [8] Not only does Garrick criticize Quin's acting for its clichéd bravado and lack of variety, but he recommends a new kind of internalized action for dramatic characters which will accommodate elements of uncertainty as well as of bluster. Suffering and doubt thus stand in Garrick's mind as active qualities and as legitimate subjects for exploration in the theater—even in a role such as Macbeth, surrounded in the trappings of a heroic tradition.

Garrick's character-descriptions in his *Essay* also reveal that both in comedy and tragedy, his resort to technical means of rendering character came very early in his approach to his roles.

To see this practical reflex in an actor is not surprising, but it is striking that in these accounts Garrick chose nonverbal moments as the clearest demonstrations of his way of drawing character. In his choice of gestures and posture for each character, he sought to suggest a psychologically complex and continually shifting personality; and in this sense, each character's physical actions—or "reactions" in our sense of the word—become the most reliable and eloquent testimony to an extreme internal state, replacing the powerful or euphonious declamation of the Restoration stage and its legacy to eighteenth-century acting. Quin's traditional emphasis on the way in which he would speak Macbeth appears to have contributed to the repetitious and awkward elements in his rendering of the character.

Garrick argued with this traditional emphasis, and as he put it later in one of his letters, "*Action, Action, Action*, are words better apply'd to ye drama than to Oratory."[9] Action, for Garrick, was an observable quantity which existed on the surface of dramatic character and whose essential meanings could be seen and understood by anyone. With the further caution in his *Essay* that "in some Cases, Passions are Humours, and Humours Passions; for the Revenges of an Alexander and a Haberdasher, may have the same Fountain, and differ only in their Currents," Garrick challenged the strict neoclassical distinction between comedy and tragedy and the wide disparity in ways considered admissable to actors of rendering characters in the two genres.[10] In sum, Garrick's species of "action" was more democratically applied than it had been during the Restoration, and more comprehensively and subtly realized than it had been by most of the practitioners of neoclassically influenced heroic acting. It is very unlikely that any of these practitioners would have equated a tragic character with a comic one, in the fashion that Garrick did in *An Essay on Acting*.

The methods by which Garrick forged physical actions into a psychologically coherent and emotionally compelling texture stand as a separate problem, and his *Essay* volunteers few of the principles which guided his creation of climactic moments for Abel Drugger and Macbeth. Nevertheless, Garrick's vivid descriptions of these characters' actions suggest that he first conceived of a role, practically, in terms of specific physical gestures at moments of peak emotional intensity, and that he then moved outward from these toward a broader sense of the character as a complete and rounded "personality." If this hypothesis is correct, a character's "action," for Garrick, was in some respects equivalent to that character's personality in its incarnation on the stage. Along these lines, Garrick's oblique testimony suggests a similarity between his action-centered image of dramatic character and the "method of physical actions" which Constantine Stanislavsky would refine nearly two centuries after Garrick published his *Essay*.

Garrick's stage shared with Stanislavsky's an extensive use of physical objects. The scenic realism of the late nineteenth century was anticipated by the domestic focus of Garrick and his age, which worked to bring more of the familiar objects of everyday life onstage than had been the case on the sparsely set Elizabethan stages or on the scenically illusionistic ones of the Restoration. In this connection, too, Garrick's innovations first as an actor, and later as a manager, worked to reduce the scale of Restoration heroes, whose painted stage-worlds conjured up images of the magnificent and boundless which appealed particularly to the baroque sensibilities of the late seventeenth century. In opposition to the Restoration's disregard for the familiar and the life-sized, especially in tragedy, Garrick made rather obtrusive use of a white handkerchief as Hamlet, expressing his triumph after the playing of "The Mousetrap"; and at the moment of his cursing Goneril as King Lear, he made a bit of business out of his angry discarding of a crutch which he had used to support his weight until that climactic moment in the production.[11] In these and other instances, Garrick granted physical action a more specific and extensive outlet than it seems to have found on English stages during the seventeenth century and into the eighteenth, when hand properties had been fewer and wings-and-border sets had followed the unlocalized Elizabethan backdrop as the means for establishing the world of the play.[12]

Through the course of the eighteenth century, settings came increasingly to rely on free-standing three-dimensional pieces, as well as on the growing use of properties and furniture to supplement the older painted, two-dimensional surfaces. Progressively, the actor's onstage environment shifted from its being one intended to showcase the scene painter's skill and the playwright's skill—embellished by the actor's facility—at evoking atmospheric effects in the text, to one which held an immediate sensory reality for the actor and so demanded physical immersion and a specific address. In this connection, Garrick's resort to physical objects as vehicles for his character-drawing worked to reduce the scale of his roles to something rather closer to that of the objects which composed their world.

Also in the way of resorting to the literal capacities of objects, Garrick once wrote a criticism to the painter, George Romney, of the artist's portrait of playwright Richard Cumberland. As Cumberland's friend, Garrick judged the painting to be too stiff and static, and he jokingly suggested to Romney that "you must give him something to do; put a pen in his hand, a paper on his table, and make him a poet."[13] Garrick's facetious choice to endow Cumberland with a "prop" in order to better capture his personality is typical of Garrick, first for its humor and second for its tendency to see and describe the world in essentially theatrical terms. Even through the jest, Garrick's confidence in the broad applicability of the stage techniques with which he was familiar is clear; and his invocation of their intrinsic dynamism suggests his larger view, which he expressed often during his tenure as a theater manager, that the stage had a practical and positive application in its moral address to the English public.

THE EXEMPLARY ACTOR

Garrick's interest in the moral obligation of theater to its audience—and his ways of capitalizing on his own upright conduct as a private citizen—marks him off from earlier actor-managers and from the leading actors whom he replaced in the public favor at the time of his debut. James Quin and Charles Macklin had each killed a man in backstage altercations, although each was later exonerated by pleading self-defense. As a young theatergoer and aspiring actor himself, Garrick must have watched both men carefully, and he incorporated features of Macklin's naturalism into his own style. But his personal background worked in several ways to distinguish him from the more rough-and-ready types who seem to have been drawn to the stage in the generation prior to his debut, whose very roughness appears to have contributed in some measure to commercial appeal.

Roughness was generally lacking and upward mobility was the model for the Garrick family well before David was born. Garrick's paternal grandfather was a French Huguenot who fled to England in 1685, in the aftermath of persecutions which had followed the revocation of the Edict of Nantes by Louis XIV. The Huguenot's first son, Peter, established a respectable career as an army officer, and in Lichfield, the provincial garrison town where David was born and grew up, the father's profession conferred a certain dignity on the whole of the Garrick family. David was able to gain a solid, if not luminous, education and, once in London, succeeded in making something of a literary reputation for himself by writing a popular afterpiece, *Lethe*, and seeing it produced in the year prior to his debut. By 1740, too, he was able to gain some personal credit and contacts in the business world through his three years of dealing as a wine merchant. His own experience, then, before his first appearances on the stage marked him as a young man of honesty, probity, and promise.

Once he chose the stage for his livelihood, his reputation and standing as an actor grew steadily as he became a more prominent, wealthy, and esteemed member of English society. Many of his contemporaries came rather quickly to trust in Garrick's personal propriety, and perhaps in consequence they showed the willingness as a group to see him depart from the traditional repertoire of the leading actor, heavily seasoned with great tragic and Shakespearian roles, and to essay characters of meaner or more ridiculous stripe. In this process, Garrick's actions as a private citizen—and the degree of his familiarity in many of London's social circles—worked to build a new distinction between his own personality and the characters he played. Almost invariably, his life as a citizen offered his audience the assurance that he did not possess the values of a reprobate like Richard III, and that he would do his best to infuse even the most corrupt of his characters with some hint of redeeming conscience.

This tendency on his part involved a significant modification of earlier notions of poetic justice. Garrick was especially fond of creating a moment of moralizing in his playing of a morally flawed character, often very near the end of the character's life within the play, in which he, in character, could be seen to share for a moment his audience's revulsion at prior actions. The most famous of these moments fell in his Macbeth, in the death speech he wrote for the character, and in his tormented playing of the tent scene and nightmare as Richard III which so captivated the audience on the night of his London debut.

Moreover, in his pride at his ability to play both Abel Drugger and Macbeth, Garrick testified to the growing philosophical belief in the potential perfectibility of all men.[14] That the lowly Abel was worthy of scrupulous refinement, repeated playing, and itemized description by the age's greatest actor argues that Garrick, in his professional capacity, reflected the changes which were transforming the size and composition of English theater audiences in the course of the eighteenth century. Not only were Garrick's audiences more socially varied than had been the audiences of the Restoration, top-heavy with courtiers and hangers-on to the court, but there seems also to have arisen a new respect for the dignity of work and for the persons such as tobacconist Abel who performed it.[15]

In the process of England's growth into a more egalitarian society, Garrick profited and flourished. His versatility as an actor stands not only as his unique personal achievement, but also as a tribute to the particular social ethic of the time, which valued a largeness of spirit and the willingness to approach other men on their own terms. In this world, the middle-class ethic was transformed into an esthetic in its application to Garrick's acting and to the revised notion of dramatic character which Garrick helped to evolve. The association of class values with esthetic ones was not new, but during the eighteenth century it worked to distinguish Garrick's acting style from that of Betterton, who had been nurtured in the values of Restoration court society and so seems to have adopted an approach to acting characterized by a more socially elitist stance.

Betterton was the leading actor of the Restoration after the death of his early rival, Charles Hart, and, like Garrick, was considered versatile by his age. It appears, though, that he was "at his best in heroic and tragic roles, although he played well some roles in high comedy."[16] Low comedy and farce were not his strengths as an actor, if he essayed these kinds of roles at all.[17] The keynote of Betterton's acting in all the surviving descriptions of it is its deliberation and dignity, and Betterton in his private life was widely held to possess these qualities.[18] His surpassing dignity, which translated itself remarkably well to the stage, was an especially valuable attribute in the tragic heroes and comic rakes he created so frequently and with such distinction at the height of the Restoration. The actor of such roles was called upon continually to elicit admiration for his characters from the audience, in preference to the sympathy and subjective identification which were to become the primary attendants of theatergoing experience in the eighteenth century.[19]

Garrick, on the other hand, could accommodate the playing of low comic parts to his sense of personal dignity, although he was criticized early in his career for undertaking such parts by people still dyed in the memory of Betterton's selective and austere repertoire.[20] Garrick was also encouraged in his early aspirations toward a broader versatility by the altered sensibility of his age, which could countenance laughing at a character, or at his situation, without feeling that it was necessarily ridiculing him. This assumption, in turn, helped to create in Garrick an acting style which could embrace characters of all types with equal facility, and which could assume that the old "humours" and "passions" were indistinguishable in some cases. Betterton, acting in an age when comic characters with the exception of the aristocratic rake-heroes of high Restoration comedy were held as social and artistic inferiors, was not likely to have achieved Garrick's distinction in low comic roles even if he had wanted to. In Betterton's time, such characters had not yet assumed the dignity automatically conferred in tragedy, because the aristocratic contingent among the Restoration audience was very influential in its tastes. Such tastes lasted long after the Restoration and remained quite resistant to the nascent impulses toward granting much dignity to persons who needed to work for a living, or who were laughable in any way.

THE ACTOR AS *PARVENU*

There are vestiges of the Restoration bias against work and nonmartial, nonerotic physical activity as unseemly in some of the early criticism of Garrick. Horace Walpole, son of the former prime minister Robert Walpole, deprecated the low humor brought out by any heavily gestural style of acting when he referred to "those excellent exhibitions of the animal or inanimate part of creation, which are furnished by the worthy philosophers [John] Rich and Garrick."[21] Theophilus Cibber, son of the poet laureate Colley Cibber and one of the actors whose style was called into question by Garrick's success, asked of Garrick's admirers, "Is not his chief talent comedy—not of genteel cast, but of the lower kind?" He then went on to add a series of more specific criticisms of Garrick's

studied tricks, his over-fondness for extravagant attitudes, frequent affected starts, convulsive twitchings, jerkings of the body, sprawling of the fingers, slapping the breast and pockets—a set of mechanical motions in constant use, the caricatures of gesture suggested by pert vivacity; his pantomimical manner of acting every word in a sentence; his unnatural pauses in the middle of a sentence; his forced conceits; his wilful neglect of harmony, even where the round period of a well-expressed noble sentiment demands a graceful cadence in the delivery.[22]

Charles Macklin added his voice to the sour chorus some years later, having little good to say about Garrick after feuding with him in the aftermath of an actors' strike which they joined to lead in the fall of 1743.[23] According to James Boaden, Macklin was fond of distinguishing himself from Garrick as an actor who "abhorred all trick, all start and ingenious attitude; and his attacks upon Mr. Garrick were always directed to the restless abundance of his action and his gestures, by which, he said, rather than by the fair business of the character, he caught and detained all attention to himself."[24] If Macklin's normative sense of what constitutes "the fair business of the character" does not conjure up images of Quin wallowing around the stage as Macbeth, it does recall Anthony Aston's description of Betterton's austere physical presence onstage: "His actions were few, but just. . . . He was incapable of dancing even in a country dance. . . ."[25] It is interesting that Macklin, long categorized as a rebel with Garrick against traditional acting, upholds the taste of the Restoration in its dislike of profuse physical action in characters of dignity. Finally, Captain Thomas Morris, writing in 1764 and with no apparent personal animosity to spur him on, still shows evidence of the persistent neoclassical bias against comedy as a form and against the more vigorous workings of the body: "Shakespeare wrote from his heart; Garrick played from his head. . . . the sudden and unnatural transition of voice; the studied and always premature start; the pantomime gesture . . . miserable expedients fit only for a booth in a fair, not for royal theatres of the metropolis."[26] Such criticisms suggest that there was something in Garrick's "action" on the stage, and particularly in its unfamiliar animation and its focus on irresolution in characters, which struck some viewers as coarse. Older images of heroism had depended more on dignity, repose, and sheer physical and vocal power, and Garrick's acting would always remain vulnerable when measured against these standards.

Thomas Davies, Garrick's first biographer and for a time an actor in his company at Drury Lane, pinpointed the cause for Garrick's failures in a handful of roles, Antony in *Antony and Cleopatra* and Othello among them. Davies felt that Garrick "admired the energy of passion more than dignity of character," and his critical opposition of "passion" to "dignity" spells out a view of acting that also dates from the Restoration. This view ascribes the greatest heroism to characters able to overcome passion through the agency of reason.[27] Such a view, with its emphasis on eloquent speaking and reasoned, metrically precise discourse, contains an inherent class bias—translated into esthetic terms—and it was a critical stance which continued on with some vehemence and frequency through roughly the first half of Garrick's career.

Horace Walpole enunciated this stance in its baldest form in a letter to Horace Mann in 1742. Viewing Garrick's sudden rise as a symptom of the degeneration which a larger playgoing public had wrought in the level of taste, he complained that "all the run is now after Garrick, a wine-merchant, who is turn'd player at Goodman's Fields. He plays all parts, and is a very good mimic. His acting I have seen, and may say to you, who will not tell it again here, I see nothing wonderful in it, but it is heresy to say so; the Duke of Argyle says he is superior to Betterton."[28] The source of Walpole's criticism we may gather from the tone of his patronizing reference to a "wine-merchant . . . turn'd player." He saw Garrick as an upstart in attempting to draw members of polite society to witness his acting; and as one of the aging Whig Augustan tastemakers, Walpole shows little willingness to hand over his prerogatives as critic to "all the run," particularly when the object of its new affection had only recently been a wine merchant. It is further interesting that Walpole, who was later to become Lord Orford, should have been surprised at the taste in acting shown by the Duke of Argyle: In regard to the capriciousness of the refined audience of which he considered himself a member, and which he was reluctant to offend, Walpole bemoans a world turned upside-down.

Nor was Walpole's opinion of Garrick to change much, as he came to know the actor better:

I dined to-day at Garrick's. There were the Duke of Grafton, Lady Rochfort, Lady Holderness, the crooked Moysten, and Dabren, the Spanish minister; two regents, of which one is Lord Chamberlain and the other Groom of the Stole; and the wife of a Secretary of State. This is being *sur un assez bon ton* for a player! Don't you want to ask me how I like him? Do want, and I will tell you. I like her [Mrs. Garrick] exceedingly; she is all sense, and all sweetness too. I don't know how, but *he* does not improve so fast upon me. There is a great deal of parts, vivacity, and variety, but there is a great deal, too, of mimicry and burlesque. I am very ungrateful, for he flatters me abundantly, but, unluckily, I know it. I was accustomed to it enough when my father was First Minister; on his fall I lost all at once.[29]

Walpole's criticism of Garrick is again couched in social terms, in his resentment at the favor and access afforded to a mere "player." We see, too, the distrust of actorly qualities when exercised in polite society, as Walpole seems to suspect the same "parts, vivacity, and variety" which served Garrick so well on the stage. But the apparent enthusiasm of the rest of the distinguished company points to Garrick's ability to minimize the so-

cial stigma directed at him as a member of a traditionally out-
cast profession. During his lifetime, he was able to gain nearly
universal social acceptance for himself, if not for his fellow actors as a group.

Walpole's impression of Garrick's personal style was shared,
with some moderation, by Samuel Johnson. Coming from the
same small town of Lichfield and having himself known Garrick as a boy and taught him at the short-lived academy at Edial,
Johnson seems always to have found it difficult to credit the adulation showered upon his former student, even as he himself
was leading a struggling existence through many of his early
years in London. Moreover, Johnson seems to have nourished
some of the older prejudice against acting, in the form of the
assumption that there was something intrinsically degrading
about the practical demands of assuming multiple foreign
identities. To those who maintained that Garrick must have felt
every passion at the same time and in the same way that he
played it, Johnson was in the habit of asserting "that Garrick
himself gave in to this foppery of feelings I can easily believe;
but he knew at the same time that he lied."[30]

Johnson echoed Walpole, too, when he found particular fault
with Garrick's ability as an actor to represent "an easy, fine-bred
gentleman."[31] On its surface, this remark may appear incredi-
ble coming from Johnson, who had a reputation for being blunt
to the point of rudeness. However, a number of Garrick's contemporaries were to join Johnson in the opinion that Garrick's
insistent busyness as an actor served to subvert his ability to realize a refined gentleman. In the midst of fulsome tributes to
Garrick, the aptly named Francis Gentleman added his voice to
the party, and his more sympathetic tone illuminates the source
of the criticism more clearly: ". . . though graceful in motion,
and very much so in attitude, he never could picture dignity,
nor attain what is called the fine gentleman, a character indeed
too languid for his active powers."[32] Through Gentleman's eyes,
we recognize that the basis for such criticism of Garrick's acting
lay in the older Restoration image of the "fine gentleman" as a
person who demonstrated his superiority in repose and intel-
lection, rather than through vulgar and anxious exertion.

It is odd that this implicitly aristocratic view of gentility could have continued on into the middle part of the eighteenth century, at a time when the middle class was gaining unprecedented authority and influence in English society. But the foremost defenders of this view seem themselves to have been members of the generally progressive and egalitarian middle orders. Such critics, perhaps, sought to recommend their own gentility by derogating members of their own class and reaffirming the essential features of a dying social ethic. Their criticism of Garrick also suggests the nostalgic appeal which older images of the fine gentleman and of his rarefied tastes still maintained at the time of Garrick's debut. In the wake of that debut, the authentic fine gentlemen of 1741 evidently found little to complain of in the actor's portrayals of them, or of other kinds of characters.[33] It was, rather, the supersensitive middle-class critics who bridled at Garrick's unseemly "activity." The notion of personal identity residing in a dignified, self-possessed man of reflection—and in somehow permanent and immutable form—was to remain a current one in contemporary critical standards well after Garrick's first appearance and the middle class' achieving of social and economic ascendancy.

Garrick, then, was not an actor for all tastes. Issues of social class and possible snobbery aside, his busyness could obtrude itself on the purity of his characterizations, and his diminutive size was certainly a handicap in roles such as Antony and Othello. On the other hand, the sort of class bias which characterizes the criticism of Walpole and Theophilus Cibber (Johnson's owes to other causes, which we shall examine shortly), did diminish toward the end of Garrick's career. The diarist Hannah More observed of one of Garrick's final Hamlets, played in the year he retired, that the actor "never once forgot he was a prince; and in every variety of situation and transition of feeling you discovered the highest polish of fine breeding and courtly manners."[34] Besides reflecting the altered dramatic tastes of his age, Garrick seems also to have embodied a change in manners and in the quality of general social access. Indeed, his own wide exposure to members of the English aristocracy may have worked some direct changes in manners at that level of society. In any case, what may have bordered on vulgarity to some in 1741 did not still do so in 1776, when Garrick retired from acting.

As Garrick won an ever-wider acceptance in polite society, his acting was praised more and more frequently for its representing that which was typical and best in humankind, rather than for its departures from previous acting styles. This makes sense, of course, to the degree that other actors began to imitate Garrick's style. From being revolutionary at its beginnings, it became something close to a standard by which all other actors were judged. But a larger process was at work, too, as his acting became a mechanism by which new ways of moving, of speaking, and of thinking about the self were brought first into prominence, and finally into fashion. The middle class in eighteenth-century England was fortunate to have had an actor, and a great one at that, as one of its most prominent representatives. The excellence of Garrick's acting, and its particular stress on sympathy, sentiment, and sensibility, gradually came to stand for the worth and dignity of an entire social movement.

The feeling of optimism which surrounded Garrick's early career owes to the actor's assumptions about the essential goodness and potential perfectibility of humankind. These beliefs marked him as typical of his time and of his class, and they were the correlatives of his sympathetic and moralizing approach to dramatic characters. Garrick's acting diverges from current notions of the sentimental, however, in the degree to which it incorporated personal initiative into its notion of goodness. Garrick's own life was itself a monument to the effectiveness of personal initiative; and his own credence in middle-class values endowed his acting with much of its force and conviction. His contemporaries ascribed his excellence as an actor to his possession of a heightened faculty for "sympathy" and to an abundance of sentiment in his nature—at least those did so who admired it. But during much of Garrick's career, such words were used to describe an active process by which one person could encounter and engage another, in life as well as in art.

Thomas Davies characterized Hamlet's "What a piece of work as a man" speech as a "beautiful description of man and his powers,"[35] and Francis Gentleman referred to the same moment in the play as the most "concise and beautiful . . . delineation of human nature as thought can conceive or words can express."[36] How different is this reading of Hamlet's short paean to mankind (which gives way quickly to bitterness) from many of those of our own time, which have considered it primarily in its subsequent development as a sarcastic expression of Hamlet's cynicism and world-weariness. Even though Davies had gone on to criticize Garrick for acting "too tame and temperate in speech and action" in delivering the lines, [37] the critics' agreement about the tone of the moment—and the criticism of Garrick's qualification of it in depicting Hamlet's wariness of Rosencrantz and Guildenstern as he uttered it—indicate the essential optimism and generous assessment of humanity which suffused Garrick's theater and his society.

Garrick's career captured the acting of a confident actor before the audience of a confident time. Let us look next at the ways in which domestic experience and the sentimental functions which attended it were at the heart of the optimistic mood which surrounded the moment of Garrick's debut, and at the ways in which these values aged, even as the actor did.

NOTES

1. Garrick received a copy of Francis Hutcheson's book from Henry Giffard, his first acting teacher. Garrick mentioned the book in his letter of October 26, 1745, to Somerset Draper; see *The Letters of David Garrick*, ed. David M. Little and George M. Kahrl (Cambridge: Harvard University Press, 1963), I, 66–67.

2. Francis Hutcheson, *An Essay on the Nature and Conduct of the Passions and Affections with Illustrations on the Moral Sense*, 3d ed. (1742; rpt., ed. Paul McReynolds, Gainesville, Fla.: Scholars' Facsimiles & Reprints, 1969); see especially Hutcheson's section VI, "Some General Conclusions concerning the best Management of our Desires, with some Principles necessary to Happiness," beginning on p. 167.

3. *The Letters of David Garrick*, II, 635.

4. *The Letters of David Garrick*, I, 28–29.

5. David Garrick, *An Essay on Acting* (London, 1744), p. 4.

6. Garrick, *Essay*, p. 5.

7. Garrick, *Essay*, pp. 7–9.

8. Garrick, *Essay*, pp. 17–18.

9. *The Letters of David Garrick*, II, 542.

10. Garrick, *Essay*, p. 5.

11. Arthur Colby Sprague, *Shakespeare and the Actors: The Stage Business in His Plays (1660–1905)* (Cambridge: Harvard University Press, 1944), pp. 159, 286.

12. Kalman A. Burnim, *David Garrick, Director* (Carbondale: Southern Illinois University Press, 1973), pp. 88–101.

13. Mrs. Clement Parsons, *Garrick and His Circle* (New York: G. P. Putnam's Sons, 1906), p. 238.

14. This belief was first expressed in coherent and comprehensive form in the works of Anthony Ashley Cooper, Lord Shaftesbury, particularly in his *Characteristics of Men, Manners, Opinions, and Times* (1711).

15. See Ian Watt, *The Rise of the Novel: Studies in Defoe, Richardson and Fielding* (Berkeley: University of California Press, 1957), especially his chapter III, " 'Robinson Crusoe,' Individualism and the Novel," which treats the elevated standing physical labor began to assume in broader sections of eighteenth-century English society (pp. 71–74).

16. Emmett L. Avery and Arthur H. Scouten, *The London Stage 1660–1700: A Critical Introduction* (Carbondale: Southern Illinois University Press, 1968), p. cvi.

17. There is little evidence of such an attempt on Betterton's part in Judith Milhous, "An Annotated Census of Thomas Betterton's Roles, 1659–1710," *Theatre Notebook*, XXIX (1975), 33–43, 85–94.

18. Avery and Scouten, *The London Stage 1660–1700*, pp. clii–cliii. Anthony Aston amended Colley Cibber's praise for Betterton in the role of Falstaff by claiming that in the part Betterton had "wanted the waggery of Estcourt, the drollery of Harper, and sallaciousness of Jack Evans"; from "Lives of the Actors," cited in *The Life and Times of That Excellent and Renowned Actor Thomas Betterton*, anon. (London: Reader, 1888), p. 121.

19. See Geoffrey Marshall, *Restoration Serious Drama* (Norman: University of Oklahoma Press, 1975), pp. 194–95, for a discussion of how admiration for protagonists was built into the assumptions of Restoration dramaturgy.

20. *The Private Correspondence of David Garrick*, ed. James Boaden (London: Henry Colburn and Richard Bentley, 1831), I, 5–6. In a letter to Garrick written in January 1742, the Reverend Thomas Newton, a friend of Garrick, wrote to the actor that:

I was almost angry with you, to see your name last week in the bill for Costar Pearmain [in Farquhar's *The Recruiting Officer*]. I am not fond of your acting such parts as Fondlewife [in Congreve's *The Old Batchelor* or even Clodio [in Colley Cibber's *Love Makes a Man*], nor should be of The Lying Valet, if it was not of your own writing. You who are equal to the greatest parts, strangely demean yourself in acting anything that is low and little. . . .

21. *The World*, No. 6, February 18, 1753; cited in *The Idea of Comedy: Essays in Prose and Verse, Ben Jonson to George Meredith*, ed. W. K. Wimsatt (Englewood Cliffs, N. J.: Prentice-Hall, Inc., 1969), p. 194.

22. Theophilus Cibber, "Dissertations on Theatrical Subjects" (London, 1759); cited in James E. Murdoch, *The Stage, or Recollections of Actors and Acting* (Cincinnati: Robert Clarke & Co., 1884), pp. 473, 477.

23. Percy Fitzgerald, *The Life of David Garrick*, rev. ed. (London: Simpkin, Marshall, Hamilton, Kent, & Co., Ltd., 1899), pp. 67–70.

24. James Boaden, *Memoirs of the Life of John Philip Kemble* (London, 1825), I, 440–43; cited in A. M. Nagler, *A Source Book in Theatrical History* (New York: Dover Publications, Inc., 1959), p. 373.

25. From Anthony Aston, *A Brief Supplement to Colley Cibber, Esq.; His Lives of the Late Famous Actors and Actresses*(1747); cited in *Actors on Acting*, ed. Toby Cole and Helen Krich Chinoy (New York: Crown Publishers, Inc., 1970), p. 114.

26. From Mr. Reuben Gold Thwaites' reprint of the *Journal of Capt. Thomas Morris*, dated "Detroit, Sept. 25, 1764," in *Early Western Travels, 1748–1846* (Cleveland, 1904); cited in C. B. Cooper, "Captain Thomas Morris on Garrick," *Modern Language Notes*, XXXII (1917), 504–5.

27. Thomas Davies, *Memoirs of the Life of David Garrick, Esq.* (London: Printed for the Author, 1780), I, 152.

28. Quoted in James E. Murdoch, *The Stage, or Recollections of Actors and Acting*, p. 456.

29. Quoted in Murdoch, *The Stage*, pp. 500–501.

30. Joshua Reynolds, *Portraits: Character Sketches of Goldsmith, Johnson, and Garrick*, ed. Frederick W. Hilles (New York: McGraw-Hill Book Company, Inc., 1952), p. 118.

31. T. H. Vail Motter, "Garrick and the Private Theatricals," *A Journal of English Literary History*, XI (1944), 64.

32. Francis Gentleman, *The Dramatic Censor; or, Critical Companion* (London: Printed for J. Bell, 1770), II, 483.

33. For examples of the early praise given Garrick and his acting by members of the British aristocracy, see *The Letters of David Garrick*, I, 31, 39.

34. Hannah More, *Memoirs and Correspondence* (1834); cited in Gamini Salgādo, *Eyewitnesses of Shakespeare: First Hand Accounts of Performances, 1590–1890* (London: Sussex University Press, 1975), p. 240.

35. Thomas Davies, *Dramatic Miscellanies* (London: Printed for the Author, 1784), III, 45.

36. Gentleman, *The Dramatic Censor*, I, 20.

37. Davies, *Dramatic Miscellanies*, III, 45.

David Garrick and His Wife, by William Hogarth. By permission of the Lord Chamberlain. Copyright reserved by Her Majesty The Queen.

2

The Language of Melting, and the Refinement of Sentimental Acting

The eighteenth-century vocabulary of sympathy, sentiment, and sensibility worked in principle at least to unite men to one another in its depiction of feelings and experience which it considered common to all. We see many of the plays and novels of the period set in a typical middle-class household, visited by members of the aristocracy, usually out of motives connected with courtship, and shared by servants whose amorous adventures run in courses roughly parallel to those of their social superiors. This domestic/romantic formula is one which argues, through reiterated images rather than through words, that even if each person's sensory experience of the world is unique, as Locke thought that it was, his fundamental needs are essentially the same as any other person's.

Although it has been qualified and narrowed as a term of literary description by the tendency of recent scholarship, *sentiment* is a term crucial to any examination of the values and assumptions which lay behind Garrick's acting. I shall try to demonstrate the ways in which sentiment was couched in a broader descriptive vocabulary and to show that Garrick's brand of sentimentalism, in its applications on the stage, represented a very broad strain in the tastes of his age. I shall also try to show how the uses of sentimentalism by an actor call for a distinction between its more practical applications and its usage as a term of literary-historical description. A spirit of sentimentalism pervaded Garrick's life and his art; and by seeking out the area of overlap between the two, we may be able to approach more closely the quality of energy which made him so compelling to watch on the stage. Let us look first at the roots of the acting tradition Garrick rejected and try to refine a sense of that which was sentimental in Garrick's style in terms of that which was not in earlier ones.

ACTING BEFORE 1741

Robert D. Hume has argued for an elaborate and attenuated transition from a Restoration or "Carolean" dramaturgy to an "Augustan" one, featuring the lapse of tragedy as an effective form for contemporary playwrights, a more benevolent view of human nature, appearances of overt moralizing, and transformations of dramatic characters into clear moral exemplars.[1] Hume feels that all of these conditions were in place by 1710 and that there exists a continuum in the development of English dramatic literature between 1660 and 1737. And yet by 1741, the year of Garrick's debut, there is no evidence to suggest that a change in acting style had emerged comparable to those which Hume and others have demonstrated at work in the drama prior to 1710. In fact, a general adherence to older acting styles presents the most conspicuous feature of the acting between 1710 and 1741; and the revolution in acting, when it did finally arrive with the emergence first of Charles Macklin and later and more convulsively of Garrick, happened within the space of several months, in contrast to the lengthy duration of changes which seem comparable in playwriting. Why does acting as an art seem to have been more retrograde than was playwriting in the generation before Garrick's debut?

Betterton's reign as England's leading actor had been unchallenged between the death of his major rival, Charles Hart, in 1683 and his own death in 1710—and he had achieved a substantial following even from the time of his debut in 1659. His career thus spanned the entirety of the Restoration and of the generation which followed it; and his prestige and skill as an actor fixed certain essential features of his own style in the popular consciousness for many years after his passing. This style had been refined at the height of the Restoration, and descriptions of it invariably pay homage to Betterton's skill as a speaker.[2] Furthermore, the virtues of an acting style which stressed speech as its primary expressive mode were not questioned at all in the years after 1710.

Betterton's speaking had been quite natural and easy, although his delivery was dignified in the extreme. His immediate successors may have tried to recreate it and failed; or they may have disguised their insufficiencies, when measured against Betterton's formidable standard, by moving toward a more musical and ornate delivery, guided that way perhaps by the growing commercial success of the opera, or even by some impulse, inchoate in nature and unrecognized and unrewarded by the audience, to incorporate sentiment and accommodate it with the essential lineaments of the old style.[3] In any case, Dudley Ryder reported in his diary in 1716 that "the manner of speaking in our theatres in tragedy is not natural. . . . Persons would call it theatrical, meaning by that something stiff and affected . . . as if they were reading a book."[4] A Swiss traveler, Henry Misson de Valborg, stated this criticism even before Betterton's death when he wrote circa 1698 of his impressions of English actors: "When they happen to go out of prose into verse, you would swear you no longer heard the same person; his tone of voice becomes soft and tender; he is charmed, he dies away with rapture."[5]

It seems that none of Betterton's major successors in tragedy, Barton Booth, Robert Wilks, and James Quin, was able to match the simplicity, naturalness, and suppleness of his delivery. Colley Cibber, writing in 1740, still regarded Betterton as unequalled, and he praised him in ways that reaffirm the virtues of the older actor's style:

There cannot be a stronger Proof of the charms of harmonious Elocution, than the many, even unnatural scenes and Flights of the false Sublime it has lifted into Applause. In what Raptures have I seen an Audience, at the furious Fustian and turgid Rants in Nat. Lee's Alexander the Great! For though I can allow this Play a few great Beauties, yet it is not without its extravagant Blemishes. . . . When these flowing Numbers came from the Mouth of a Betterton, the Multitude no more desired Sense to them, than our musical Connoisseurs think it essential in the celebrate Airs of an Italian Opera. Does this not prove, that there is very near as much Enchantment in the well-govern'd Voice of an Actor, as in the sweet Pipe of an Eunuch? . . . In all his Soliloquies of moment, the strong Intelligence of [Betterton's] Attitude and Aspect, drew you into such an impatient Gaze, and eager Expectation, that you almost imbib'd the Sentiment with your Eye, before the Ear could reach it.[6]

In Cibber's opinion, neither Booth, who had modeled his acting on Betterton's, nor Wilks, who had styled his from Mountfort's, "ever came up to their Original . . . if Wilks had sometimes too violent a Vivacity, Booth as often contented himself with too grave a Dignity."[7] Criticisms of Quin from his contemporaries are even less flattering. Colley Cibber did not deign to mention Quin in his *Apology*, and Colley's son, Theophilus Cibber, deprecated Dennis Delane by claiming that "either from an Imitation of Quin or his own natural Manner, he has a sameness of Tone and Expression, and drawls out his Lines to a displeasing Length."[8] Even given these liabilities, Theophilus adds that Quin and Delane were "without Competitors" at Drury Lane and Covent Garden, respectively, in 1741, the year in which declamation was finally to be challenged.[9]

It was not the substance of declamation which had grown stale as much as its practice. Writing later in the century, Thomas Davies recalled the appearance in 1731 of an aged Mr. Boman, who as "the last of the Bettertonian school" had given his audience a chance to "guess at the perfection to which the old masters in acting had arrived."[10] Remarkable actor that he was, Betterton seems to have succeeded in intimidating his successors to the point that they were afraid to depart very far or very fundamentally from the self-contained, euphonious style he had perfected. The audience, too, appears to have applied a normative standard to Betterton's successors, much in the fashion of neoclassical esthetics. Another peculiar feature of the years following Betterton's death was the extreme disparity alluded to by Dudley Ryder between the vocal delivery of comic actors, who spoke in something like ordinary conversational tones, and the singsong of the tragic players.[11] Colley Cibber was himself the foremost comic actor of this period, and despite his long claim to literary distinction as the originator of domestic comedy,[12] his acting both in comedy and in tragedy was marred by what in modern parlance would be called "commenting," a condition evidenced by Davies' comparison of Garrick's "Bayes" in the Duke of Buckingham's *The Rehearsal* to Cibber's earlier characterization.[13]

Cibber also undertook tragic roles, and with almost uniformly unfortunate results. Aaron Hill criticized Cibber's Richard III for its "low mincing curtails of magnanimity . . . a succession of comic shruggings . . . the distorted heavings of an unjointed caterpillar."[14] This sort of awkward and unassimilated physical expression reminds us of Garrick's description of Quin as Macbeth in the dagger scene. When Cibber attempted a comeback in 1736 in *Papal Tyranny*, he was ridiculed for the "unnatural swelling of his words."[15] Nor was Cibber's lack of distinction in the declamatory tradition an obstacle to his passing it along whenever he could. Writing in 1750, Garrick complained of an appearance by a granddaughter of Cibber's, who had recently played Alicia in Rowe's *Jane Shore*: "The Young Lady may have Genius for ought I know, but if she has, it is so eclips'd by the Manner of Speaking ye Laureat has taught her, that I am affraid [sic] it will not do—We differ greatly in our Notions of Acting (in Tragedy I mean) & If he is right I am, & ever shall be in ye wrong road."[16]

Betterton's long preeminence, together with an absence of worthy challengers to his mantle in tragedy, may have succeeded in fixing the memory of an ideal declaimer, and of the emotional simplicity and depth which had characterized his acting. Although clearly different kinds of plays had begun to be written as early as the 1690s, anticipating the sorts of changes which would later coalesce into sentimentalism, no new acting style seems to have evolved to address the demands of plays containing a more benevolent view of human nature and characters intended to serve as moral examples.[17] For example, Theophilus Cibber, by all accounts a worse actor in tragedy than his father—and doubtless instructed by him in much the same way as Colley would later instruct the granddaughter—was left to create the role of George Barnwell in Lillo's prototypical domestic tragedy, *The London Merchant* (1731).

By 1741 Quin had been holding forth for some years, Wilks, Booth, and Colley Cibber having left the stage in the early 1730s. Earlier in the same year that Garrick made his debut, Charles Macklin created a stir with his passionate and sympathetic portrayal of Shylock, and so amended a comic-villainous tradition of playing the character which had been passed along from earlier Restoration actors by Thomas Dogget, who acted exclusively in comedy.[18] The novel, as a new literary form, had succeeded in gathering such disparate impulses as the benevolism of Richard Steele, the moral seriousness of Lillo, and the *comédie larmoyante* of Nivelle de la Chausée in France into treatments of the critical importance of society and environment in determining individual behavior. In some senses, the novel appears to have anticipated the theater in consolidating and popularizing Locke's sensationism and Shaftesbury's flattering image of human nature into something which manifested a broad commercial appeal. As G. S. Rousseau has observed, there seems to have occurred in the novel a sort of "catching up" to the philosophical developments of the late seventeenth century.[19] All of this—the championing of domestic virtue in *The London Merchant*, the return to Terentian gentility and benevolism in the comedies of Steele, the evolution of a new literary form which celebrated the moral propriety and economic ascendancy of the middle class, and the passage of the Licensing Act in 1737, effectively banning from production plays with controversial political content—contributed to the climate in which Garrick made his debut.

THE WORKINGS OF SYMPATHY

It is notable that Garrick's debut came not in a new, explicitly sentimental role, but in a much older one. As Richard III, Garrick seems to have surprised his unsuspecting audience by infusing the character with touches of vulnerability and weakness. This approach to the character parallels that of Macklin to Shylock; and such colors were especially surprising in a character which had been the recent property of Colley Cibber, with his writhing and smirking, and of Quin, with his stentorian reserve. Garrick, in contrast to these earlier characterizations, wove a thread of introspection into the character. According to Thomas Wilkes: "Whenever he speaks of his own imperfection he shows himself galled and uneasy. . . . 'Then I am like no brother, &c.' Garrick in all these places shews by his acting the cross-grained and splenetic turn of Richard the Third; he shews you how the survey hurts him: whereas I have seen some people here smile upon themselves, as if well pleased with their own appearance. . . . "[20] As Richard, we see Garrick going to some lengths not only to endow the character with psychological complexity, but to draw the audience into sympathy with an obviously troubled character. This latter choice is a remarkable one given the broad manner in which Richard had been played before him.

The ability to inspire a sympathetic response to even the most morally tainted or positively villainous characters became one of Garrick's trademarks, and it differentiated him from the more brittle, objectified, and typological acting which had been the rule for some years prior to his and Macklin's appearances in 1741. His Macbeth, his King John, his Hastings in Rowe's *Jane Shore*, and his Lothario in *The Fair Penitent* are other instances of characters who appear unsympathetic in their literary incarnations—the first two of them murderers and usurpers, and the last two reckless, selfish, and irresponsible rakes—but which Garrick reinterpreted through the prism of sympathy. In the cases of Macbeth and King John, Garrick bathed the characters in paralyzing self-doubt, and out of this matrix created moments of impulsive and self-destructive lashing out. Hastings and Lothario he dyed in romantic passion, and this succeeded in softening somewhat the overtly exploitative sides of these characters.[21]

Garrick's own discussion of King Lear in one of his letters further demonstrates the extent to which he seems to have approached all of his roles in a resolute spirit of sympathy:

Lear is certainly a *Weak* man, it is part of his Character—Violent, old & *weakly* fond of his Daughters . . . his Weakness proceeds from his Age (fourscore & upwards) & such an Old Man full of affection, Generosity, Passion & what not meeting with what he thought an ungrateful return from his best belov'd Cordelia, & afterwards real ingrati-

tude from his other Daughters, an audience must feel his distresses &
Madness which is ye Consequence of them—nay I think I might go
farther, & venture to say that had not ye source of his unhappiness
proceeded from good qualities carry'd to excess of folly, but from vices,
I really think that ye bad part of him would be forgotten in ye space
of an Act, & his Distresses at his Years would become objects of Pity
to an Audience.[22]

With Lear, as with Lothario, Hastings, Macbeth, and King John,
Garrick appears to have concerned himself with elements of
sympathy in his characters, especially in the degree that he felt
the danger of a lack of sympathy in the tradition of the roles as
they had been played before him. In any case, it is hard to
imagine a Lear acted in our own times which could approach
Garrick's in the nearly total lack of "vices" ascribed to the character of the crusty old king. If, as it seems, twentieth-century
critics and audiences tend to see King Lear in terms of the old
man's pride and rashness, Garrick did so in terms of the character's extreme age, his physical weakness, and his absolute de-
pendence on his offspring.

   This sympathetic component of Garrick's acting was at the core
of his revision of earlier and more conventionally heroic styles.
There exists a connection between "sympathy" and the manifestations of sentiment in his acting, when we examine the sorts
of qualities of character which would have aroused sympathetic
identification among an eighteenth-century audience, sensi-
tized as it was to matters of the family and of the heart. If Betterton had thrived through his ability to inspire admiration for
the peerless characters he played, Garrick did so through the
arousal of sympathy by appearing often unthreatening and vulnerable onstage. We shall look a bit later at the role his small
stature and unprepossessing voice played in his expressive capacity, but both of these physical characteristics stand in contrast to those of the heavyset and deep-voiced Betterton, and
of his less talented imitator, Quin.

GARRICK AND SENTIMENT

   In a letter to playwright John Home concerning Home's
tragedy, *The Fatal Discovery*, Garrick expressed satisfaction that

in his reading the play aloud he had been able to draw "tears last Night in great plenty from my Wife, & a very intimate friend of ours. . . . I read it with all my Powers & produc'd that Effect, wch I wd always Wish to do in reading a work of Genius."[23] In a later letter to the Reverend John Hoadly, one of Garrick's closest friends, the actor exclaimed at Hoadly's reaction to Cumberland's *The West Indian*: "I rejoice that you wept at ye *West Indian*: I shall tell him [Cumberland] of yr Criticisms, & I'm sure he will profit by them."[24] Judging from such statements as these, it seems that Garrick may have used the tears of his familiars as an index of the popular and commercial potential of works he was considering for production. It also seems clear enough that he was not mocking or patronizing his wife and his old friend in their lachrymose reactions to sentimental plays, and that he assumed these reactions to be humane ones, and generally typical of those which the works might elicit, or were already eliciting, at Drury Lane.

The prevailing scholarly opinion for some years, based on some of Garrick's writings and remarks hostile to sentimental playwriting in his own day, has been that he was antagonistic to the appearance of sentiment in any form, though in stage comedy in particular.[25] Indeed, Garrick did occasionally deride sentiment in its extreme forms, notably in his prologue to Goldsmith's *She Stoops to Conquer* (1773).[26] Several of his letters, such as the one to his brother Peter in 1762, take a similarly dim view of the appearance of sentiment in comedy. He wrote to Peter as he waited to go onstage as a character in William Whitehead's *The School for Lovers*, a new play that year: "I Don't appear in ye Play till the beginning of the 2d when Sr John Dorilant (that's ye Name) makes his Entrance—and a fine, polite, Sentimental, Windling Son of a Bitch it is—a great favorite of ye Ladies, & much admir'd by the Clergy. . . . Humbug for Nine Nights. . . ."[27] Garrick may have been responding here to the quality of the play, in which he acted only one more time after its successful run during its first season: On the other hand, Garrick was under no obligation to produce plays he did not like, except perhaps that of commercial expedience. Or he may have been writing to his brother in a perverse and "cross-grained" spirit, with his gratuitous cursing of so clearly exemplary a character as Sir John. Writing in 1770 to the Reverend Charles Jenner, Garrick urged the playwright to "think of giving a Comedy of Character to ye Stage—one calculated more to make an Audience Laugh, than cry—the Comedie Larmoyante is getting too Much ground upon us."[28] This excerpt may represent a more balanced image of Garrick's attitude toward sentimentalism, as something which had a place in comic playwrighting but which had been exploited beyond the limits of actorly resources and commercial appeal in the eight years which had elapsed since the appearance of *The School for Lovers*.

In the letter to Jenner, Garrick lays the responsibility for sentimental comedy squarely at the feet of the French, as he distances himself and the English public from it as *comédie larmoyante*. As an actor, he may also have been regretting the tendency of sentimental plays—as the form evolved—to homogenize characters into molds virtually identical from play to play; in fact, reservations on this score may have been activated in his harsh description of Sir John Dorilant by that character's resemblance to the "Heartly" of his own afterpiece, *The Guardian*, written three years before *The School for Lovers*.

Garrick's attitude toward arousing sentimental response in tragedy was quite different, as we have seen already in his joyous reaction to his wife's tears on her hearing Home's *The Fatal Discovery* read. Similarly in the case of Cumberland's sentimental comedy, *The West Indian* (1771), Garrick was ecstatic at John Hoadly's tearful response upon seeing the play, although instances of sentiment in the Cumberland work may have been redeemed for Garrick by its sensible, generous, and topical humanitarianism.[29] Emotion was not always invoked overfrequently and for its own sake by sentimental playwrights and actors, but it could be enlisted as well in the service of plays such as Cumberland's seen as socializing influences. Writing once to Elizabeth Montagu on a day when he was to play the aged father Lusignan in Aaron Hill's *Zara* (1735), Garrick described his relationship with one of Montagu's friends: "I am always kissing Miss Gregory's hand & will make her cry if possible tonight."[30] It is unlikely that he would have brought up the subject of Miss Gregory's tears in a frivolous way to Elizabeth Montagu, an old friend and one of the best-read Englishwomen of the century.[31] It is also doubtful that Garrick would belittle his ability to call forth tears as Lusignan, which was one of the roles he prized most highly, playing it fifty-six times during his career and at least once every season between his first appearance in the role in 1753–54 and his retirement.[32] To John Home concerning Home's tragedy *Agis* (1758), in which Garrick was to take the role of Lysander, the actor passed along the news that "Mrs. Garrick presents her best compliments to you; she has cried at you already. You have written some passages in these three acts, more like Shakespeare than any other author ever did."[33] Given his association of Home with Shakespeare as a sentimental playwright, it is not surprising that Garrick produced and acted in two of Home's plays—and that he looked to apply the same kind of sentimental appeal to Shakespearian roles that he demonstrated at work in his letters treating contemporary sentimental pieces in which he felt some personal stake.

Garrick's inclusion of Shakespeare among the ranks of sentimental playwrights of the stripe of Home and Cumberland offers evidence of the broader meanings attached to the word *sentiment* by the critics of Garrick's day. It was an article of faith that Shakespeare, as the poet of nature, had chosen to concentrate on the same sorts of wholesome concerns which Garrick's contemporaries deemed primary and universal. Along these lines, Samuel Johnson's tribute to Shakespeare in his "Preface to Shakespeare's Plays" (1765) is typical:

His persons act and speak by the influence of those general passions and principles by which all minds are agitated, and the whole system of life is continued in motion. . . . It is from this wide extension of design that so much instruction is derived. It is this which fills the plays of Shakespeare with practical axioms and domestic wisdom. . . . It will not easily be imagined how much Shakespeare excels in accommodating his sentiments to real life, but by comparing him with other authors.[34]

Garrick was not alone in associating Shakespeare with sentimental expression; but more importantly, his view and Johnson's represent the prevailing critical stance that the sentimental framework was one which had applications beyond the boundaries of historical period, nationality, and genre. Whether the word *sentiment* appeared, as in Johnson, or it did not, eighteenth-century critics as a group concentrated on domestic or romantic experience in plays, on intensified emotional responses by characters in soliloquy, and on such sympathetic responses as these moments aroused among audiences. What resulted was yet another instance of the prevailing critical tendency to judge Shakespeare's work in terms of the period's own sense of priority. Elizabeth Montagu was only adding her voice to the party when she affirmed that "Nature and sentiment will pronounce our Shakespeare to be a mighty Genius."[35]

The nonliterary uses of the word *sentiment* have been slighted, too, in several of the revisionist treatments of the sentimental strain in eighteenth-century English dramatic literature. Dating from Allardyce Nicoll's and Arthur Sherbo's studies in the 1950s,[36] there has followed a tendency to minimize the role of sentimentalism in plays of the period because of connotations of the maudlin and insincere which it conjures up more than two hundred years after its first vogue. Such recent critics as Robert D. Hume and Richard Bevis have agreed with Nicoll's contention that during the eighteenth century "almost every writer was infected more or less by its [sentimentalism's] spirit, yet pure sentimentalism was not popular and the number of perfectly unadulterated sentimental comedies hardly exceeds half a score."[37]

This view ignores the much wider application which sentimentalism found on eighteenth-century stages. There is evidence of sentiment in Garrick's productions of plays written prior to the eighteenth century, in the tone and content of virtually all contemporary tragedies written before the end of his career, and in the ways that any piece for the stage could be transformed through the agency of Garrick's acting and the assumptions which lay behind it. We read, for instance, an account of Garrick's King Lear from one Dr. Fordyce:

Those exquisite touches of self-reproach for a most foolish and ill-requited fondness to two worthless daughters, and for the greatest injustice and cruelty to one transcendently excellent. Those restless complaints of aged and royal wretchedness, with all the mingled workings

of a warm and hasty, but well-meaning and generous soul, just re-
covering from the convulsion of its faculties through the pious care of
a worthy, but injured child and follower; till at length the parent, the
sovereign, and the friend, shine out in the mildest majesty of fervent
virtue. . . .[38]

Dr. Fordyce justifies his sentimental response to this scene by
associating its progress with that of "fervent virtue," and it seems
that the more he feels as he watches, the more he affiliates himself, through the sympathetic mechanism, with the virtues of the
aged king. Another account of Garrick's Lear demonstrates the
fascination of the period for external signs of strong feeling,
and the tendency to catalogue these in solemn fashion. The
anonymous writer of "An Examen of the New Comedy Called
the Suspicious Husband" addressed himself directly to Garrick,
in praise of the actor's rendering of "Hear, Nature, hear!" (*King
Lear* I.iv.):

You fall precipitately upon your knees, extend your Arms—clench your
Hands—set your Teeth—and with a savage Distraction in your Look—
trembling in all your Limbs—and your Eyes pointed to Heaven . . .
begin . . . with a broken, inward, eager Utterance; from thence rising
every line in Loudness and Rapidity of Voice, [and at last] bursting
into Tears.[39]

This account captures Garrick's characteristic resort to the expressive powers of gesture before he had to speak climactic lines
of dramatic text, or as moments of punctuation interspersed
throughout a longer speech. It is the very elaborateness of his
gestural overlay which stirs the audience into sentimental response. In the sentimental framework, too, physical manifestations of feeling, such as kneeling or weeping, were regarded as
more true and spontaneous responses than were words; and
Garrick's own expressive strength in facial mobility and bodily
ease suited him ideally to the requisites of sentimental expectation and response—in the degree, at least, that it had not gone
toward defining them in the first place.

   In addition to its being revisionist as an approach to acting,
Garrick's gestural emphasis would seem to run counter in its
spirit to the elaborate verbal signals of feeling provided by

Shakespeare, and it may also help to explain the extreme conventionality and generality of much eighteenth-century playwriting. Following Garrick's debut, it began to matter less what the playwright wrote because the writer would have expected many actors to supply their own bodily accompaniment to the dramatic text in any case. Physical catalogues of grief, of joy, or of rage became just as profuse and conventionalized in the theater as did the expression of sentiment in words. But in the hands of a great actor such as Garrick they could be kept fresh and riveting, too. In this sense, sentimentalism grounded the sources of the "feelings" firmly in the body. Betterton's relatively still and upright style had combined with his expressive emphasis on speaking to create an image of the Restoration hero as reasoning, dignified, and self-possessed. Garrick's style created quite a different profile for the dramatic hero, as the creature of feeling, of impulse, and of the body.

Arthur Friedman has argued the existence of a distinction between sentimental treatment of dramatic characters and the evocation of a sentimental response from the audience.[40] But just as sympathy was distributed among the character, the actor, and the audience, so was sentiment shared—as a physical and literally *feeling* experience—when it was disposed on the stage most effectively. The authenticity of sentiment which Garrick's Lear aroused in his audience is patent; and the actor himself was not immune to identifying with the role, in certain of its features. One story had it that following Garrick's final performance as King Lear, the actress playing Cordelia, Miss Younge, had requested Garrick's blessing and that he had obliged her backstage with all the soberness and gravity of the character.[41] Davies reports that when he was on his deathbed, Garrick "told Mr. Lawrence, that he did not regret his being childless; for he knew the quickness of his feelings was so great that, in case it had been his misfortune to have had disobedient children, he could not have supported such an affliction."[42] The weight assumed by familial experience seems disproportionate to many commentators in our own time, but such experience offered the most vivid and compelling theatrical models to Garrick and to the major part of his audience, as well as the foundation for the sentimental responses they shared.

THE QUALITIES OF SENTIMENTAL ACTING

Garrick's sentimental treatment of Shakespearian roles can only make us wonder what resulted when he essayed roles in contemporary plays expressly tailored to his expressive strengths. It may also cause us to regret that more accounts of his non-Shakespearian tragic characterizations have not survived him. One of the most detailed of the accounts which have survived describes his performance of Hastings in Rowe's *Jane Shore*, when having just received word of his death sentence together with the news that the woman he had tried to ravish had unwittingly helped to implicate him in a treasonous plot, Garrick's Hastings spoke the line, "Now mark! and tremble at Heaven's Just Award." And then he

got perfectly calm and composed, and these lines were uttered in a deep affecting tone that was truly heartrending; and in "Here, then, exchange we mutually forgiveness", he contrived by a little pause, and then kneeling with her, to get rid of grief and every distracting thought; he held one of her hands, in his, while he made the address to heaven, and did it with great energy and firmness; and in the passage, "Farewell! good angels visit thy afflictions", he left her again in tears, got close to the wing, spoke the last two sentences with uncommon feeling, and made a great *exit*. The applause lasted long, for half the house did not expect to see him any more. But he returned with his guard, went over to Alicia, tenderly took her hand, then turned and waved the guard to retire a little, which they did. He then led her farther off again as if to speak in private, and delivered the petition for Jane Shore comparatively in a whisper, 'till he came to the Line of "O, shouldst thou wrong her", where he swelled his cadence; but immediately subsiding once more, into a whisper, he left her and got again to the wing. They looked at each other for some time with heart-rending grief, and he, after a pause, gave the passage, "Remember this", in the tone of a man expiring. . . . The "last warning of a dying man" had taken such hold of Miss Young[e] and the audience that nothing more could be said or done with effect.[43]

Recurrent in the accounts of Garrick in sentimental roles are his focus on the external signs of emotion, his retardation of pace, and his ability to add one heightened effect to another to create moments of sustained emotional intensity. In Hastings, as with Macbeth and Abel Drugger, Garrick found a way of playing against, and so varying, the surface of intense emotion by delivering much of his final speech at very low volume. Joshua Steele reported that he adopted a similar approach to the acting of Hamlet's "To be or not to be" soliloquy.[44] Such interpretive choices make sense if we measure them against Garrick's lack of a powerful stage voice and in conjunction with the emphasis and energy he devoted to the purely pantomimic requirements of climactic moments.

His own imaginative engagement with such moments is evident in several of the remarks about acting which appear in his letters. He once made as his excuse for misplacing a caesura in a line from Macbeth[45] that "when ye mind's agitated, it is impossible to guard against these Slips"; and in the same letter he defended his placement of another caesura, in the form of a sigh, at Hamlet's "I think it was to see [. . .] my mother's wedding" (I.ii.) with the statement that "I really could not from my feelings act it otherwise."[46]

In these instances, the melting sensation aroused by sentiment has caused Garrick to experience a sense of himself as the characters so intense as to momentarily remove his ability to distinguish between them and himself. The sentiments in each case are accompanied by affective responses to domestic or nearly domestic situations—in the first example by Macbeth's revulsion at the idea of killing his patron and mentor, and in the second by Hamlet's shame at his mother's hasty remarriage. Garrick's own feelings stand clearly in sympathetic relationship to those of the characters he impersonates, and his mention of "slips" in the case of Macbeth suggests his assumption that feeling and technique can at times be mutually exclusive, a view which challenges the notion of artistic form propounded by neoclassicism in the image of "the mirror held up to Nature." Garrick's attitude also prefigures the Romantic resistance to inherited or traditional forms of expression as fetters to the release of subjective feeling in art.

Garrick's "slips" characterize his departures from a metrically faithful reading and from Betterton's speaking in "numbers," but his use of a word which connotes "mistake" also suggests his ultimate confidence that form and feeling *could* be reconciled. Garrick seems to believe that an actor can use sentiment, if he is sufficiently careful and disciplined, as a means of humanizing the formal requirements of character and of verse, even as he felt he had done in placing the caesura where he had in the line from Hamlet.

Arthur Sherbo has pointed to "repetition and prolongation" as two of the characteristic features of sentimental playwriting.[47] The appearance of such devices in a dramatic text will spur any sensible actor to search for variety in his characterization, especially in the degree that he is asked to enact passages which he himself can recognize as repetitious and prolonged! If in some measure Garrick's style introduced a significantly greater portion of sympathy and sentiment into acting at the time of his debut, he may afterward have been encouraged toward further elaborations of physicality, of silence, and of his interpretive emphasis on the richness of domestic experience by the refinements of contemporary sentimental playwrights. To judge him by his interest in the plays of John Home and Richard Cumberland, Garrick felt a sort of reciprocity existed between his acting and the uses of sentiment in many of the leading dramatic works of the day. The existence of such reciprocity would argue against Richard Bevis's recent hypothesis that "the sentimental comedy may have been primarily a reading phenomenon whose foothold in the theater was tenuous."[48] Even if this were true, the foothold of sentimental tragedy on the stages of the time was very firm indeed.

The tenacity and vitality of sentimentalism in the drama worked to inspire frequent attacks on it, and it is an odd fact that sentimental touches recur in some of the most famed and successful "anti-sentimental" comedies of the last one-third of the eighteenth century: in Hugh Kelly's *False Delicacy* (1768), in the couple of Sidney and Miss Marchmont, who although they never play a scene together and are subordinate to other more lively and less principled characters, are paired together in the final round of marriage making which ends the play; in *She Stoops to Conquer* (1773), in the couple of Hastings and Miss Neville, each of whom lacks sentimental diction but whose self-contained and self-aware behavior contrasts with the more volatile courtship between Young Marlowe and Kate Hardcastle; in *The*

School for Scandal (1777), in which Charles Surface and Maria
are finally united as the least morally tainted young people in
the play; and most clearly perhaps in Sheridan's *The Rivals*
(1775), which among the preceding plays contains the only examples of patently sentimental scenes between Julia and Faulk-
land. In all of these works, though, sentimentalism acts as a ref-
erent, setting off the behavior of the more upright, honorable,
and romantically committed characters from that of their more
impulsive, manipulative, and unconventional brethren. In short,
the attempt at nonsentimental playwriting in the 1760s and 1770s
was made in terms of a steady reference to sentimental models.
Although these models were subordinated in many plays of the
period to characters and situations which seemed more vital and
original, the sources of that vitality and originality lay precisely
in the vividness, immediacy, and familiarity of stage behaviors
seen as more commonplace and more "feeling." Toward the end
of Garrick's career, then, the sentimental and the nonsentimental were working in tandem, the one serving to define the other
and give it life in its onstage incarnations, even as the masque
and anti-masque had done in the Jacobean period.[49]

In Garrick's mind, "sentiment" did not need to be ubiquitous
in order to be effective. In fact, in his review of Colman the
Elder's *The English Merchant* (1763), he implied that sentimental
expression demanded complementary moments of laughter in
order to sustain its effectiveness onstage: ". . . a vein of comedy runs through the whole play . . . yet the distress of *Amelia*
and her father make the comic muse *raise her voice* in many of
the scenes and give a variety which is not to be met within the
lower Species of the drama, or in that, which the French call
Comedie Larmoyante."[50] It was not sentiment to which Garrick
objected so much as the sameness of tone and response which
often attended its exercise in dramatic literature, and he took
great care in his acting, in his advice to playwrights, and in his
own playwriting to avoid a lack of variety. He may even have
believed in the sort of melting reaction which Laurence Sterne
described in a letter to Garrick, arguing the interrelationship of
laughter and tears: "I laugh till I cry, and in the same tender
moment cry till I laugh."[51] This alternation of emotions may
have outstripped tears alone as Garrick's image of the ideal in
sentimental response.

THE FRUITS OF SENTIMENTALISM

Nowhere did Garrick use the word *sentiment* in a favorable context, although he seems to have done with his acting that which he refused to do in his pronouncements on the theater. In his writing, and in his public functions generally, he may have been reacting against the rather broad and corrupted meaning which the word *sentimental* assumed in popular usage during the later years of his career.[52] But he also grew accustomed to tributes to himself such as that offered by the Reverend Charles Jenner, who dedicated his *The Man of Family* (1771) to Garrick "not to the manager or actor . . . but to the man of feeling and the scholar."[53]

It is clearly Jenner's assumption that learning and feeling, far from being mutually exclusive, in fact enhance one another, in depth as well as in quality. In this connection, the word *sensibility* may have felt more satisfactory to Garrick than *sentiment* in its evocation of feeling tinctured with learning and humanitarianism, and for its connoting a more enlightened and active stance toward the world. The actor referred once to his reluctance to kill animals in a letter to Peter Fountain: "I could make you laugh [at] mine and my Wife's Sensibility—I go even father than Mr Lloyd, I [will] not kill ye hare, no more than ye Greyhound."[54] As he had demonstrated in his descriptions of Abel Drugger and Macbeth, feelings were pertinent in a character only insofar as they precipitated sympathy in the audience and action in the character. The connotations of passivity which "sentiment" assumed later in the eighteenth century has been carried over into our own time,[55] but there was little of the passive either in Garrick's way of capturing sentiment on the stage or in the corollaries of sentiment through the larger dramatic actions of the plays he produced.

R. F. Brissenden has observed that before 1777 dictionaries generally defined *sentiment* as "thought,"[56] and that " 'sensibility,' 'sentiment,' and 'sympathy' were terms with precise meanings in the newly developing sciences of physiology and neurology."[57] Although the usage of sentiment grew more broad and vague in the popular parlance as the eighteenth century moved toward its close, it was employed much more precisely in learned circles. Garrick's own preference for *sensibility* may reflect the savor of the physical and the sensory which *sentiment* lost progressively as it became ever more associated with emotional and spiritual phenomena. We have already seen the ways in which his acting was rooted in a kind of physicality that worked to remove it from earlier declamatory styles; and this development may have come as a practical extension of the tendency which had begun with Locke among English philosophers toward challenging Platonic distinctions between the workings of the mind and those of the body. According to Brissenden, the idea of sentiment incorporated the synthetic notions of "mental feeling" and "emotional thought,"[58] and these formulations remind us of Garrick's own reference to the "bodily Emotions" in his *Essay on Acting*.[59] Such usages suggest a belief in the soul and mind as "feeling" entities like the body, and in the emotions not only as the triggers to physical action but as themselves the products of it.

And so, from its recent association with science and physical sensation near mid-century when Garrick made his debut, the word *sentiment* acquired progressively the flavor of "sham, the shallow, and the insincere" which had worked to alter its meaning a good deal by the end of Garrick's career.[60] This is the meaning of the word which Garrick began to react against by the late 1750s, and the scope of his reaction extended itself to other critics as the century went on. In the wake of the French Revolution, "sentiment" among English critics came to be associated with a dangerous, anarchic ascendancy in the sway of the emotions over the moderating powers of reason.[61] With the advent of Romanticism, too, came both the valuing of feeling over thought in some quarters and the relegating of "sentiment"— as an older word with sensory overtones which many Romantics deemed coarse—to a reduced and at times risible place in the critical vocabulary.[62]

Arthur Sherbo has argued that the appearance of the word *sentimental* applied to a *play* did not occur until 1750, in the prologue to William Whitehead's *Roman Father*.[63] If this is true, the word's broadening meaning, from its earlier and more refined usage, may have come partly as the result of its exposure to a wider population. But the way that the word changed from a precise, clinical, and scientific one into its loose and bawling cousin also reveals something of the temper of the times in which the alteration occurred. What grew in currency between the time of Garrick's debut and his exit from the stage was a general interest in the causes and manifestations of strong emotion, and a prevailing belief that the act of expressing emotion was good for its own sake and as a near-equivalent to action.

Garrick himself helped to revise *The Roman Father* extensively before its premiere production in 1750, and he created its title character, Horatius.[64] In these connections he may well be implicated in the popular abuse of the word *sentiment* which he later derided. By the 1760s, parodies of sentimental plays began to find their way to the stage in increasing numbers, but rather than marking the end of the sentimental impulse, these only testify that sentimental playwriting and acting were flourishing, and so offered inviting targets for ridicule. Garrick himself wrote at least one parody of sentimentalism in *The Guardian* (1759), but the vigor and coherence of his criticism of sentimental abuses is qualified by the equivocal nature of the play's denouement, which manufactures a final reconciliation and engagement between the previously disaffected and tortured sentimental couple.[65] Such equivocation is also testimony to Garrick's eminently commercial sensibilities, and his inclination as manager in the late 1760s and 1770s was to produce and write prologues for antisentimental plays such as Goldsmith's and Sheridan's, while continuing to perform heavily sentimentalized heroes and to mount productions of sentimental plays in some profusion. It was profitable for Garrick to capitalize on sentiment, and it was also profitable for him to criticize it.

Garrick's collaboration with George Colman the Elder on *The Clandestine Marriage* (1766) offers further evidence of his temporizing on the matter of sentimentalism. The comedy, like Goldsmith's and Sheridan's plays, weds sentimental modes to nonsentimental ones. The central sentimental couple, Fanny and her Lovewell, are plagued by an assortment of comic types whose function is to obstruct the course of the couple's true love. These blocking characters include Lord Ogleby, an aged roué who courts Fanny himself; Sterling, the grasping father resisting his daughter's romantic inclinations; and Mrs. Heidelberg, Fanny's social-climbing aunt, who wishes only for the girl to marry an aristocrat and so elevate the family's social standing. Elizabeth Stein and others have felt that because Garrick himself seems not to have contributed to the Fanny-Lovewell component of the play, he must have been using his own contributions, in the form of the blocking characters, to deride and undercut the more overt expressions of sentiment which the play contains.[66] This view seems to ignore the matter of Garrick's interest in creating a unified work, not to mention his commercial motives toward a favorable public response to the play. Indeed, it is possible that Garrick and Colman agreed that their diverse contributions to the play—if so diverse they were—would work in a complementary way, and so serve the success of their collaboration. Garrick's relations with Colman were generally friendly, after all, and the only falling-out they had during the time that they were working on the play came because Garrick finally refused to act Lord Ogleby himself.[67]

As an actor, Garrick may have been drawn to criticize sentimentalism in contemporary dramatic comedy by its tendency to make many dramatic characters seem alike and by its failure to live up to Shakespeare's *corpus* as compelling works for the stage. As a critic and manager, he became aware of the growing need to temper sentimental expression with less idealized elements in the name of providing sufficient variety to his audience. As it evolved, sentimentalism was a dramatic form which fairly begged for complementary expressions; but it could be complemented, and it was, without sacrificing its efficacy. It was precisely the effectiveness of sentimental material in draining an audience of emotion which created the need for comic relief in the theater. Still another mark of its success as a form of dramatic expression lay in the extent to which it was incorporated into nineteenth-century melodrama, lending to the later form its morally exemplary characters and its emphasis on arousing strong feelings in connection with romantic or domestic circumstances.

Sentimental acting, then, presupposed the existence of a sympathetic component in dramatic characters, focused on familial or romantic situation, and sought to arouse the most intense emotional response that it could, for as long as it could. Laughter as well as tears could attend its exercise, even in trag-

edy. Samuel Foote, a satirist and cynic who in general deplored
Garrick's manner of playing King Lear, was stunned nevertheless by the effects Garrick was able to achieve in scenes late in
the play:

. . . wherever quick Rage is to be express'd, no Actor does the Poet
so much Justice, nor is he less successful in tincturing all the Passions,
with a certain Feebleness suitable to the Age of the King, the Design
of the Author, and the raising in the Minds of the Audience a stronger
feeling, and Compassion for Lear's Suffering. . . . Nor can I leave him
without my particular Thanks for the Entertainment he has given me
at his Recovery from Madness, and Recollection of Cordelia. . . .[68]

That so skeptical and superficially unsentimental a critic as Foote
was moved by Garrick's Lear offers evidence of the subliminal
power which sentimental expression held for the audiences of
the day.
In 1769 Garrick wrote to Helfrich Peter Sturz, in a passage
which has been widely quoted since, in which he tried to distinguish between

a great Genius, and a good Actor. The first will always realize the feelings of his Character, and be transported beyond himself, while the
other, with great powers, and good sense, will give great pleasure to
an Audience, but never
    —pectus inanitor angit
    Irritat Malis & falcis, terroribus implet Ut Magus. [Horace, Epis-
tles, II.ii.211–13: "With airy nothings wrings my heart, inflames, soothes,
fills it with vain alarms like a magician."][69]

The idea of an actor's being "transported beyond himself" an-
ticipates the Romantic view of the mystical powers of artistic experience; but Garrick separated himself from later notions of
the transporting capacity of extreme subjectivity by grounding
his acting in an appeal to values held to be universally apprehensible, and by his constant resort onstage to the world of the
senses. Garrick's "transport" conveyed him to another part of
this world: The transport of Romantic actors carried them to
another world entirely.
The kind of acting which resulted from Garrick's mixing sen-

timent with sensation distinguished itself not only from its successors but from its predecessors, too, in its theoretical admission of the role of "transport" in artistic endeavor. Betterton had claimed, through his phantom biographer, Charles Gildon, but nevertheless consistent with neoclassical strictures on the imagination and with what we know of his own acting style, that "tho the Passions are very beautiful in their proper Gestures, yet they ought never to be so extravagantly immoderate to transport the Speaker out of himself."[70] It was precisely this kind of transport, with the actor melting into the character for brief ecstatic moments, that Garrick sought to create for himself and his audience when he was on the stage.

Robert D. Hume, Richard Bevis, and Geoffrey Marshall have all distinguished in recent years between *sentiment* and *sensibility*, and they have agreed that the latter term is the more legitimate in its broad application to the dramatic literature of the eighteenth century.[71] They have also agreed on a definition of *sensibility* in the drama as the clear embodiment of an idealizing impulse at work on the eighteenth-century English stage, in its combination of a benevolent view of human nature and the conscious shaping of dramatic characters as moral examples to the audience which watched them.

I do not find *sensibility* an entirely satisfactory word to apply to Garrick's acting. Using sympathy as its leading edge, that acting sought unashamedly to lengthen and intensify emotional response among its audience, and in tragedy at least it claimed the evocation of tears as the ultimate proof of its effectiveness. This aim *was* sentimental, in Garrick's sense if not in our own, because it was enacted in the spirit of sincerity and conviction on Garrick's part, and not merely as an exercise in manipulation. This is the facet of eighteenth-century sentimentalism which distinguishes it from the grosser calculations of the nineteenth-century melodrama.

Hume and Bevis have also agreed that a conservative movement overtook English playwriting by the end of the first decade of the eighteenth century, rendering plays of the following Augustan period for a time less bold and inventive than they had been during the Restoration and its immediate aftermath.

Such a view ignores the eventual success of the sentimental movement and of the cult of sensibility at resurrecting vital and effective expression on the stage, apparently because the revival did not produce a dramatic literature which has endured in any great quantities into twentieth-century repertoires.[72]

But the reasons for the vitiation of the English drama which occurred around 1710 lay not only in the quality of the plays produced then, but in the ways those plays were acted, too. Garrick spearheaded the movement toward regenerating the English stage and parts of its traditional repertory in his transforming of a passive and largely theoretical and abstract image of human behavior into a more active one, predicated on the social and moral utility of the nuclear family and of laissez-faire capitalism. If this seems a lofty claim for an actor to make to historical impact, it testifies also to the need of English society during Garrick's lifetime to find tangible, visible affirmations of its collective beliefs. Tears and other signs of extreme emotions did not represent weakness to Garrick and his audience, but stood rather as an energy which could be channeled constructively into dynamic and altruistic action.

The actor wrote once to John Hoadly in his concern for protecting the memory of Hoadly's physician-playwright brother, Benjamin, from the threat of defamation some years after Benjamin had died: "My Eyes are full of Water, while I write to You, but this is not a token of Weakness, but resolution."[73] It was this attitude and all it stood for which worked to counter the stagnant condition of the stage in the generation which had followed Betterton's death, and which in diluted and corrupt form evolved into the nineteenth-century melodrama. If it did not inspire also a new golden age of English playwriting, at least it resuscitated many of the older plays in the repertoire and so contributed to the adulation of Shakespeare which was to continue on through the nineteenth century and into our own day. In the next chapter we shall explore some of the reasons why Garrick's acting may have suited Shakespeare's plays better than contemporary ones; but the amount of attention focused on the *manner* of playing during his career seems to have worked to reduce his audience's awareness of the merits and even the actual content of works written while he held the stage.

NOTES

1. Robert D. Hume, *The Development of English Drama in the Late Seventeenth Century* (Oxford: Clarendon Press, 1976), pp. 5, 491–92.

2. For accounts of Betterton's skill at speaking, and his emphasis on it, see Charles Gildon, *The Life of Mr. Thomas Betterton* (London: Printed for Robert Gosling, 1710), *passim*; and Colley Cibber, *An Apology for the Life of Colley Cibber* (London: Printed by John Watts for the Author, 1740), pp. 59–71.

3. See *The Revels History of Drama in English*, vol. V, *1660–1750*, ed. John Loftis (London: Methuen & Co., Ltd., 1976), pp. 288–95; and Emmett L. Avery, *The London Stage, 1700–1729: A Critical Introduction* (Carbondale: Southern Illinois University Press, 1968), pp. xix, lxxi–lxxiii.

4. *The Diary of Dudley Ryder 1715–1716*, ed. William Matthews (London: Methuen, 1939), p. 360; cited in Philip Highfill, Jr., "Performers and Performing," *The London Theatre World*, ed. Robert D. Hume (Carbondale: Southern Illinois University Press, 1980), p. 164.

5. Henry Misson de Valborg, *Memoirs and Observations in His Travels over England* (1719), p. 221; cited in Bertram Joseph, *The Tragic Actor* (London: Routledge and Kegan Paul, 1959), p. 86.

6. Colley Cibber, *An Apology for the Life of Mr. Colley Cibber* (1740), pp. 63–66.

7. Colley Cibber, *Apology*, pp. 336–37.

8. Theophilus Cibber, *An Apology for the Life of Mr. The' Cibber* (Dublin, 1741), p. 172.

9. Theophilus Cibber, *Apology*, p. 170.

10. Thomas Davies, *Dramatic Miscellanies* (London: Printed for the Author, 1784), II, 100.

11. See John Harold Wilson, "Rant, Cant, and Tone on the Restoration Stage," *Studies in Philology*, LII (1955), 592–98; and Arthur Colby Sprague, "Did Betterton Chant?" *Theatre Notebook*, I (1946), 54–55.

12. This claim has lately been disputed by Robert D. Hume in *The Development of English Drama in the Late Seventeenth Century*, p. 308.

13. See chapter 6 in this study for a discussion of the ways in which Garrick's Bayes departed from Cibber's. A salient description of the differences between the two appears in Davies, *Dramatic Miscellanies* III, 303–4.

14. Aaron Hill (and William Popple), *The Prompter (1734–1736)*, ed. William W. Appleton and Kalman A. Burnim (New York: Benjamin Blom, 1966), p. 6.

15. Davies, *Dramatic Miscellanies*, I, 40.

16. *The Letters of David Garrick*, ed. David M. Little and George M. Kahrl (Cambridge: Harvard University Press, 1963), I, 158.

17. See Hume, *The Development of English Drama*, pp. 9–10, *passim*.

18. *Revels History of Drama, vol. V, 1660–1750*, pp. 146, 248.

19. See G. S. Rousseau, "Nerves, Spirits, and Fibres: Towards Defining the Origins of Sensibility," in *Studies in the Eighteenth Century*, vol. III, ed. R. F. Brissenden and J. C. Eade (Toronto: University of Toronto Press, 1976), p. 142.

20. Thomas Wilkes, *A General View of the Stage* (London: Printed for J. Cooke, 1759), p. 237.

21. Contemporary accounts of Garrick as Macbeth can be found in Arthur Murphy, *The Life of David Garrick, Esq.* (London: J. F. Foot, 1801), I, 99, *passim*, and in Murphy's letter to Garrick in *The Private Correspondence of David Garrick*, ed. James Boaden (London: Henry Colburn and Richard Bentley, 1831), II, 363; in Francis Gentleman, *The Dramatic Censor; or, Critical Companion* (London: Printed for J. Bell, 1770), I, 106–7; in Jean Georges Noverre, *Letters on Dancing and Ballets* (New York: Dance Horizons, 1966), pp. 84–85; and in Davies, *Dramatic Miscellanies*, II, 125–76. Accounts of his King John fall in *Dramatic Miscellanies*, I, 102, *passim*; of his Hastings in "Garrick and His Contemporaries" (pp. 73–79), collected by George Daniel, in the Folger Shakespeare Library, and cited at length by Cecil Price in his *Theatre in the Age of Garrick* (Oxford: Basil Blackwell, 1973), pp. 6–13; and of Garrick's Lothario in Francis Gentleman, *The Dramatic Censor*, I, 273–74. Descriptions of Garrick's performances as Macbeth and Lothario appear also in George Winchester Stone, Jr., and George M. Kahrl, *David Garrick: A Critical Biography* (Carbondale: Southern Illinois University Press, 1979), pp. 549–59, 525–27.

22. *The Letters of David Garrick*, II, 682–83.

23. *The Letters of David Garrick*, II, 614.

24. *The Letters of David Garrick*, II, 739.

25. See Dougald MacMillan, "David Garrick as Critic," *Studies in Philology*, XXXI (1934), 81–82; and Richard Bevis, *The Laughing Tradition: Stage Comedy in Garrick's Day* (Athens: University of Georgia Press, 1980), pp. 148–49.

26.

Excuse me, sirs, I pray—I can't yet speak—
I'm crying now—and have been all the week! . . .
Pray would you know the reason why I'm crying?
The Comic Muse, long sick, is now a-dying!
And if she goes, my tears will never stop;

For as a player, I can't squeeze out one drop. . . .
Poor Ned [Shuter, the actor] and I are dead to all intents,
We can as soon speak Greek as sentiments! . . .
I give it up—morals won't do for me;
To make you laugh I must play tragedy. . . .

27. *The Letters of David Garrick*, I, 351.

28. *The Letters of David Garrick*, II, 690.

29. See Joseph Donohue, *Dramatic Character in the English Romantic Age* (Princeton: Princeton University Press, 1970), pp. 95–113, for a discussion of Cumberland's humanitarian interests in *The West Indian*.

30. *The Letters of David Garrick* III, 931.

31. See Stone and Kahrl, *David Garrick*, pp. 419–26, for a treatment of Garrick's dealings with Elizabeth Montagu.

32. See Leigh Woods, "David Garrick and the Actor's Means: A Revolution in Acting-Style, in Relation to the Life of the Times,"(Ph.D. dissertation, University of California, Berkeley, 1979), Appendix F (p. 393).

33. *The Letters of David Garrick*, I, 270.

34. Samuel Johnson, "Preface to Shakespeare's Plays" (1765; rpt. Menston, Yorkshire: The Scolar Press Limited, 1969), p. ix.

35. *An Essay on the Writings and Genius of Shakespeare* (Dublin, 1769), p. 17.

36. Allardyce Nicoll, *A History of English Drama, 1660–1900*, vols. II and III (Cambridge: The University Press, 1952); Arthur Sherbo, *English Sentimental Drama* (East Lansing: Michigan State University Press, 1957).

37. Nicoll, *A History of English Drama*, vol. II, p. 128. For concurring views, see *Revels History of Drama*, vol. V, *1660–1750*, pp. 66–69; Robert D. Hume, "Goldsmith and Sheridan and the Supposed Revolution of 'Laughing' Against 'Sentimental' Comedy," in *Studies in Change and Revolution: Aspects of English Intellectual History*, ed. Paul J. Korshin (Menston, Yorkshire: The Scolar Press, 1972), pp. 237–76; and Bevis, *The Laughing Tradition, passim*. Especially valuable in Bevis's book are his summaries of the sentimental tradition in chapter 3, "The Muse of the Woeful Countenance" (pp. 43–63), and of the history of critical reactions to sentimentalism which appears in his appendix (pp. 237–48).

38. *The Private Correspondence of David Garrick*, I, 158.

39. Cited in Arthur Colby Sprague, *Shakespeare and the Actors: The Stage Business in His Plays (1660–1905)* (Cambridge: Harvard University Press, 1944), p. 286.

40. Arthur Friedman, "Aspects of Sentimentalism in Eighteenth-Century Literature," in *The Augustan Milieu: Essays Presented to Louis A.*

Landa ed. Henry Knight Miller et al. (Oxford: The Clarendon Press, 1970), p. 247.

41. Percy Fitzgerald, *The Life of David Garrick*, rev. ed. (London: Simpkin, Marshall, Hamilton, Kent & Co., Ltd., 1899), p. 429.

42. Thomas Davies, *Memoirs of the Life of David Garrick, Esq.* (London: Printed by the Author, 1780), II, 348–49.

43. Cited in Cecil Price, *Theatre in the Age of Garrick* p. 13; from material collected by George Daniel and titled "Garrick and His Contemporaries" (pp. 73–79), in the Folger Shakespeare Library.

44. Joshua Steele, *Prosodia Rationalis*, 2d ed. (London, 1779), p. 47. Steele tells us that in contrast to the style of a hypothetical "ranting actor, swelled with *forte* and softened with *piano* he [Garrick] delivered [it] with little or no distinction of piano and forte, or as a musician would say, *sotto voce*, or *sempre poco piano*."

45.

> "Heaven's cherubim horsed [. . .]
> Upon the sightless couriers of the air. . . . " (I.vii.)

46. *The Letters of David Garrick*, I, 351.

47. Sherbo, *English Sentimental Drama*, pp. 32–37.

48. Bevis, *The Laughing Tradition*, p. 33.

49. For a discussion of the masque and anti-masque as complementary forms, see Stephen Orgel, *The Jonsonian Masque* (New York: Columbia University Press, 1965), pp. 118–23, 129–31, 133–39, 158–69.

50. *Monthly Review*, XXXVI (1763), 225; cited in Sherbo, *English Sentimental Drama*, p. 150.

51. Cited in Rufus D. S. Putney, "Laurence Sterne, Apostle of Laughter," in *Eighteenth-Century English Literature: Modern Essays in Criticism*, ed. James L. Clifford (London: Oxford University Press, 1959), p. 274.

52. See Geoffrey Marshall, *Restoration Serious Drama* (Norman: University of Oklahoma Press, 1975), pp. 212–13.

53. Cited in Bevis, *The Laughing Tradition*, p. 30.

54. *The Letters of David Garrick*, III, 1293.

55. See R. F. Brissenden, " 'Sentiment': Some Uses of the Word in the Writings of David Hume," in *Studies in the Eighteenth Century*, vol. I, ed. Brissenden (Toronto: University of Toronto Press, 1968), p. 107; and R. F. Brissenden, *Virtue in Distress: Studies in the Novel of Sentiment from Richardson to Sade* (New York: Barnes and Noble, 1974), chapter 2, " 'Sentimentalism': An Attempt at Definition," pp. 11–55.

56. Brissenden, " 'Sentiment,' " p. 90.

57. Brissenden, *Virtue in Distress*, p. 39.

58. Brissenden, " 'Sentiment': Some Uses of the Word . . . ", p. 95.
59. Garrick, *An Essay on Acting*, p. 5.
60. Brissenden, " 'Sentiment': Some Uses of the Word . . . ", p. 107.
61. Brissenden, *Virtue in Distress*, p. 49.
62. See Bevis, *The Laughing Tradition*, pp. 240–41.
63. Sherbo, *English Sentimental Drama*, p. 2:

> Nay even each Moral, *Sentimental*, Stroke,
> Where not the Character but the Poet Spoke.
> He lopp'd, as foreign to his chaste Design;
> Nor spar'd an useless tho' a golden Line.

Sentimental is the only word not set in italic characters in the first edition of *The Roman Father*.
64. *The Plays of David Garrick*, ed. Harry William Pedicord and Fredrick Louis Bergmann (Carbondale: Southern Illinois University Press, 1980), V, 352–61.
65. Further discussion of *The Guardian* follows in chapter 5 of this book.
66. See Elizabeth P. Stein, *David Garrick, Dramatist* (1938; rpt. New York: Benjamin Blom, 1967), pp 238–41; Joseph M. Beatty, "Garrick, Colman and *The Clandestine Marriage*," *Modern Language Notes*, XXXVI (1921), 129–41; and Fredrick Bergmann, "David Garrick and *The Clandestine Marriage*," *PMLA*, LXVII (1952), 148–62.
67. *The Letters of David Garrick*, II, 481–83.
68. Samuel Foote, *A Treatise on the Passions* (London: C. Corbett, 1747; rpt. New York: Benjamin Blom, 1971), pp. 22–23.
69. *The Letters of David Garrick*, II, 635.
70. Gildon, *The Life of Mr. Thomas Betterton*, p. 86.
71. Hume, "Goldsmith and Sheridan and the Supposed Revolution," p. 256; Bevis, *The Laughing Tradition*, p. 231; Marshall, *Restoration Serious Drama*, p. 213.
72. This omission is especially evident in Hume, "Goldsmith and Sheridan and the Supposed Revolution," pp. 237–76.
73. *The Letters of David Garrick*, II, 739.

3

Sentimentalism in Practice in Garrick's Repertoire

What sorts of roles conformed to Garrick's sentimental definition of dramatic character? Which categories of dramatic characters performed actions he deemed appropriate for representation on the stage and compelling to his audience?

This chapter examines Garrick's roles according to their broad historical provenance, approaches the groups which emerge as manifestations of values central to the ages which produced them, and, finally, considers these values in the shapes which they seem to have assumed in Garrick's mind and in the ways they influenced his choice of roles. Several of these groupings of plays contain values which left them well-suited to Garrick's approach to dramatic character; a few others held to values inimical to the actor and his society. Not surprisingly, Garrick chose to play roles from the former group and to avoid, largely, roles from the latter. To some extent, too, Garrick's acting exerted a homogenizing effect on the roles which he acted, and his characteristic interpretive emphases worked to render plays and characters from rather diverse periods of English dramatic literature similar in the forms that they assumed on the stages of his time. Behind this entire discussion lies the assumption that it was Garrick's personal assessment of any period of dramatic literature—rather than its "objective" standing or its absolute worth in the light of literary history—which determined his own

Garrick *(far left)* as Horatius in *The Roman Father,* with Spranger Barry as Publius Horatius, Mrs. Ward as Valeria, and Mrs. Pritchard as Horatia. From the Art Collection of the Folger Shakespeare Library.

repertoire and, to a considerable extent, those of other English theaters during his tenure as manager at Drury Lane.

Garrick's roles fall into five groups, if the plays which contain them are divided according to the dates of their original composition, as they are in the appendix:

1. Elizabethan, Jacobean, and Carolinean, 1588–1642[1]   23 roles
2. Restoration, 1660–88   4 roles
3. Post-Restoration, 1688–1714   26 roles
4. Early Georgian, 1714–37   4 roles
5. Post-Licensing Act through Garrick's Retirement, 1737–76   39 roles

                                                                   total   96 roles

The paucity of Garrick's roles in two major periods of English dramatic literature is striking. What are the features of his and his audience's tastes which can explain this profile?

RESTORATION ROLES

We have already seen some of the ways in which Restoration society and taste were antithetical to the values underlying Garrick's style. It is notable that when he was in only his second season on the stage, Garrick refused to take the role of Pinchwife in Wycherley's salacious *The Country Wife*.[2] When he adapted the play himself some years later, he removed all illicit sexual contact from it and primly retitled the work *The Country Girl*.[3] Contemporary morality could apparently accommodate plays containing violence and double entendre, but it could not abide one which celebrated and, indeed, rationalized extramarital sexual intercourse. In Garrick's time, the merest mention of illicit sex in contemporary plays was subject to attack for its straining the limits of polite taste, and when illicit sexual acts were committed within the plot of contemporary works, penance and remorse were expected of the offending characters. These latter occurrences are frequent in plays written during the generation which followed the Restoration, and it is not coincidental that twenty-six of Garrick's roles, several of them among his most frequently performed, came in plays from this period.

Restoration tragedies fell almost completely out of theater repertories well before Garrick's debut, with the exception of a few late-Restoration plays showing evidence of the processes of benevolizing and moralizing which Robert D. Hume has demonstrated at work in the last two decades of the seventeenth century.[4] Reasons for the nearly total collapse of interest in Restoration heroic tragedy, in particular, owe to the ways in which the protagonists of these plays were drawn.[5] In play after heroic play, during the rather short life of the form, the hero appears as a fundamentally rational but spectacularly intemperate and autonomous figure. This profile, of course, was not one which suited these plays to Garrick's priorities as an actor, and the general lack of affinity that such characters had with shifting tastes had manifested itself even before the Restoration ended. Nevertheless, remnants of the rashness and dynamism of the protagonists in heroic tragedy remained conspicuous in the character-drawing practiced by tragic playwrights in the generation which followed the end of the Restoration, as the counterpoints, in effect, to expanded uses of pathos and to the sympathetic and often helpless heroines of the "she-tragedies."

Garrick appeared in two plays each by Otway, Southerne, and Rowe, the first a late-Restoration writer and the last two products of the immediate post-Restoration period. All of these men, however, drew protagonists which qualified the impulsive heroism of tragic heroes during the high Restoration. In the first place, not all of their leading characters were male; and even male protagonists in their plays showed a new vulnerability to the forces of romantic love. Increasingly, a total vulnerability to romantic love became a humanizing and transcendently admirable quality. Leading characters in the plays of Otway, Southerne, and Rowe still show, as a group, many of the older imperatives toward combativeness and an exalted self-image, but they demonstrate also the influence of a sensibility which by the time of Garrick's debut produced the refined comic heroes of Richard Steele and the domesticated tragic ones of George Lillo. The higher value given to romantic love rendered the lubricity and combativeness of many Restoration protagonists distasteful to the audiences of the next century and so removed the leading dramatic forms of the high Restoration from consideration for revival during Garrick's career.

Garrick's only role in a Restoration comedy came as Bayes in the Duke of Buckingham's *The Rehearsal* (1671). Not only are there no elements of bawdry in this play, differentiating it from many of the Restoration comedies of manners, but its action consists of an extended satire of the diction and the conventions of heroic tragedy. The role of Bayes was written by Buckingham in order to lampoon John Dryden (among others), at the time the most successful exponent of the heroic form. In this way, Garrick refitted an older play in order to recommend, in roundabout and whimsical fashion, newer images of heroism and social accountability which rendered as outmoded not only the older heroes, but also the style in which they were acted.

We shall look a bit later at the more particular professional uses to which Garrick put his characterization of Bayes during his first season on the London stage.

EARLY GEORGIAN ROLES

Playwriting of the Early Georgian period failed in general to improve upon earlier dramatic models. The original form of political satire which it refined as its most important contribution to the history of dramatic literature was most delightfully embodied in John Gay's *The Beggar's Opera* (1728). Gay's work, in turn, was so successful that it succeeded in spawning a number of imitations, both in spoken and in ballad-opera treatments. These ultimately grew so bold and abusive as to provoke passage of the Licensing Act in 1737, directed particularly against the savage political plays of Henry Fielding and effectively banning the production of plays with explicit, topical political content. Together with the sympathetic approach to acting brought to the stage by Macklin and Garrick some four years after its passage, the Licensing Act succeeded also in moderating the sorts of personal attacks which were still mounted in plays from time to time throughout Garrick's career. With the practice of sentimental acting, too, and in the absence of topical and allegorical content in works produced after 1737, audiences were encouraged, in effect, to attend more closely to details of character, motivation, and feeling and less closely to any practical or political applications which might have been found in the plays they watched.

Alvin Kernan has contended that authentic forms of dramatic satire have as distinctive features a plot which brings no change or development to the world of the play, and a hero who can storm and rage endlessly but who is ultimately powerless to affect either his surroundings or himself.[6] Inherent in the more minutely psychological style of Garrick's acting is the notion that characters can grow and change in the course of the play which contains them. This impulse dovetails with the fundamental assumptions of the capacity for personal growth and reform which characterized many plays written following the advent of sentimentalism as a philosophical system in the early years of the eighteenth century. The satires of Garrick's day, besides ignoring political issues, are much more generous in spirit than their Early Georgian antecedents, and they show more confidence, as a group, in their capacity to reform their targets through the force of their own example.[7]

As the joint consequence, then, of the period's lack of distinction in upholding traditional tragedy and of the newly revised notions of satire which rendered many of its most interesting plays unproduceable, Garrick played only four roles in plays written during the Early Georgian period. One of these was a farce by Fielding, *The Mock Doctor*, which had been made over from Molière's *Le médecin malgré lui* and was devoid of political address; another came in the Vanbrugh-Cibber *The Provoked Husband*, which was completed by Cibber two years after Vanbrugh's death in 1726, from an uncompleted manuscript abandoned by Vanbrugh a generation before; another Garrick role was drawn from Aaron Hill's *Zara*, adapted from Voltaire's *Zaire*, a great success on the French stage; and the last Early Georgian role came from David Mallet's *Eurydice*, a conventional verse-tragedy which looked backward in its style to the modified heroic models of Southerne and Rowe. From this survey, it is clear that Garrick found roles in plays from the Early Georgian period which avoided political satire and which drew their inspiration from earlier or neoclassically influenced dramatic models. Similar varieties of conservatism manifest themselves in Garrick's selection of roles from the late Restoration and his contemporary period as well.

ELIZABETHAN, JACOBEAN, AND CAROLINEAN ROLES

His selection of parts from the English Renaissance drama was a bit more adventurous, but it was squarely in line with the broad features of eighteenth-century sensibility. Within Garrick's repertoire of Shakespearian roles, the extreme popularity of Benedick with the audience of the time may be explained by the prominence of courtship and marriage as themes which determine the action of *Much Ado about Nothing*.[8] Garrick increased receipts by first appearing as Benedick in 1749, immediately

following his marriage to the Austrian dancer, Eva-Maria Veigel, and by performing it thereafter as a celebration of his well-
known uxoriousness.

The presence of King John and the bastard Faulconbridge
from *King John*, of Posthumus from *Cymbeline*, and of Leontes
from *The Winter's Tale* among Garrick's other Shakespearian roles
may seem surprising, particularly when they are assessed in the
absence of such roles as Brutus, Cassius, Coriolanus, Prince Hal,
and any among the list of Shakespeare's clowns. The tastes of
his age and his own proclivities seem to have fixed on the domestic, familial, and sentimental situations in each of these now
less-frequently produced plays: on the obstacle presented by the
boy-prince, Arthur, to King John's attempt to cling to his ill-
gotten throne; in the lack of consequence of an illegitimate birth
in the heroic behavior of Faulconbridge; on the mistaken jealousy of Posthumus, who comes to believe that he has been be-
trayed by his beloved Imogen; and on the warm, fatherly attri-
butes of the chastened Leontes, whose tyrannies were totally
excised in Garrick's adaptation of the play, which commences
with the fourth act of the original version.[9] Of course, elements
of the sentimental figure even more prominently in *Romeo and
Juliet*, particularly in Garrick's adapted version which included
a death-duet between the two lovers, written by the actor himself.[10] It is not surprising, therefore, that two productions of the
play ran concurrently in London during the 1750–51 season,
when Garrick competed with the handsome Spranger Barry for
critical attention and commercial reward as his rival Romeo.

Garrick's two roles in plays by John Fletcher indicate the interest in emotion for its own sake and in facile and improbable
turns of plot which eighteenth-century taste held in common
with the Jacobeans'.[11] Fletcher's style of writing also contains
many of what Joseph Donohue has called "reactive" tendencies
in the drawing of dramatic character,[12] and this qualification of
earlier, bolder varieties of heroic action featured in Elizabethan
plays runs parallel to the modifications of Restoration heroism
which we have noted in both the comedy and the tragedy of
the late- and post-Restoration periods. Garrick altered the pair
of Fletcher's plays in which he took roles in ways calculated to
enhance elements of the sentimental lying nascent and largely

unelaborated within the works in their original forms, and also in order to minimize elements of satire and sexual innuendo which Fletcher's pieces had contained in measures too large to suit eighteenth-century tastes.[13]

The brief Carolinean period continued the Jacobeans' general impulse toward qualifying the dynamism of earlier Renaissance heroes. Garrick's adaptation of James Shirley's *The Gamester* (1634) and his playing of the leading rake-reformed are again consistent with his and his period's interest in refining elements of the moralized and sentimental, lying tempting and accessible within plays from earlier periods of English dramatic literature. Indeed, the role of Wilding in Shirley's original stands as a prototype for Colley Cibber's later repentent rake-heroes, as a womanizer and compulsive gambler tricked by his loving wife into reforming his errant ways.[14]

Even when his Elizabethan, Jacobean, or Carolinean roles were not imbued in sentiment in either their original or their adapted forms, Garrick's acting seems often to have moved them in that direction. Hannah More identified "filial love" as the central motive in Garrick's Hamlet, as "the great point from which he sets out, and to which he returns; the others are all contingent and subordinate to it, and are cherished or renounced, as they promote or obstruct the operation of this leading principle."[15] Two of the key moments in his performance of King Lear—namely, his curse of Goneril and his touching of one of Cordelia's tears as it trickled down her cheek late in the play—represent a marked strain of sentiment in his interpretive tendencies as an actor, and such moments were highlighted in the degree that they were treasured by audiences and singled out for praise by contemporary critics.[16]

POST-RESTORATION ROLES

In the light of Garrick's impulse to qualify harsh satire and socially autonomous and unsympathetic heroes, the frequency of his roles in the plays of the generation which followed the Restoration should come as no surprise. In addition to the total of four tragedies by Southerne and Rowe, Garrick also appeared in a number of comedies of the period: in *The Provoked*

Husband, the Vanbrugh-Cibber product; in one play by Richard Steele, father of benevolism in dramatic character; two each by Susannah Centlivre, by Vanbrugh himself, and by William Congreve (and not including Congreve's only tragedy, *The Mourning Bride,* in which Garrick also took a role); and four each by George Farquhar and Colley Cibber. All of these plays, including the original version of *The Provoked Husband,* were written between 1693 and 1714, and they survived in Garrick's time by mixing lively and complex Restoration plots with a new emphasis on the regenerative power of romantic love and the sanctity of marriage. In these plays, hotheads are cured of their obsessive pride and honor-driven jealousy, self-indulgent men are separated from their vices, and rakes are converted to fidelity. All of these feats are accomplished by heroines who remain steadfastly loyal to their flawed but fundamentally good men.

Post-Restoration comedy maintained a critical attitude toward low-comic characters as one of its legacies from the Restoration; but it employed low-comic characters in rather greater numbers than the Restoration had done, and it expanded the social range and diversity of such types in a way which departed from the Restoration's more socially homogeneous and exclusive comedy of wit. In addition to his leading jealous-heroes, dissipated bullies-made-gentle, and rakes-reformed,[17] Garrick took on one role as a cuckold, one as a comic dullard, two as servants, two more as petty tyrants, and five as fops.[18] Something of a nostalgic spirit seems to have surrounded Garrick's playing of this latter group of mostly minor roles; and the plays which contain them were viewed either with distaste, by those among Garrick's contemporaries horrified at the presence of a leading actor in "low" roles, or with delight by a larger group who appear to have welcomed the chance to measure their own benevolence and broad-mindedness against the vestiges of the more judgmental Restoration theater.

Many of these post-Restoration plays remained favorites throughout Garrick's career. Perhaps as gestures of modest reaction against their own relatively narrow tastes, Garrick's audiences sometimes welcomed the remnants of bawdry which survive in a number of the plays. Francis Gentleman, writing in

1770, disapproved of several indecent references in contemporary productions of *The Beaux' Stratagem*, but we gather from his account that his dim view of the proceedings did not represent the opinion of the majority of the playgoers:

. . . and both the ladies [Mrs. Sullen and Dorinda] rather call a blush upon the cheek of modesty, when one says—"you can't think of the man, without the bedfellow[,] I find." To which the knowing young lady replies—"I don't find any thing unnatural in that thought; while the mind is conversant with flesh and blood, it must conform to the humours of its company? [*sic*]" Another passage not very defensible, is—"mine spoke the softest moving things—mine had his moving things too? [*sic*]" —This reply is generally delivered with such an illustrative emphasis, that there needs no ghost to tell what the character, or at least the actress means; I wish this arch mode of expression, as it is called, was reformed all together; and it soon would be, if public resentment, instead of applause attended it.[19]

This passage offers evidence of the sliding scale which the eighteenth-century audience used to judge the moral content of the plays which it watched. If the play was older, it seems, indecent references might be tolerated; but a much more rigid standard was applied to contemporary works, and it is this standard which Gentleman applied, in an unconventionally retrospective way, to *The Beaux' Stratagem*. Robert D. Hume has expressed wonderment at such an audience's ability to "cheerfully swallow camels by the herd in old plays while choking over the veriest gnats in new ones."[20]

Garrick's contemporaries had a definite taste for the sexually suggestive, and they seem to have had a difficult time reconciling this taste with their general sensibility. The widespread reluctance of eighteenth-century critics to address the disjunction in taste which Hume has noted seems to have arisen as the function of collective embarrassment. A certain degree of prurience seems often to attend attempts to impose a rigid or universal moral standard, and this appears to have been the case during Garrick's career.

The post-Restoration characters which remained longest in Garrick's repertoire were Archer in *The Beaux' Stratagem*, Sir John Brute in Vanbrugh's *The Provoked Wife*, and Don Felix in Cent-

livre's *The Wonder*.[21] Each of these characters shows some redeeming feature which works to remove it from the taint of lust
in the case of Archer, of neglect and boorishness in the case of
Brute, and of unfounded jealousy in the case of Don Felix.
Archer, for all his randiness, saves Mrs. Sullen from robbers and
rescues her from her suffering in an unhappy marriage; Sir John
acquires a measure of humanity and devotion after having been
forced to appear in court dressed as a woman; and Don Felix
is taught to moderate his rashness by his patient fiancée, Vio-
lanté. Each of these transformations is accomplished in the name
of love and for the sake of a more equable and durable marriage; each change is also squarely in line with the more mutable characters and the reformative powers of sympathy refined
as features of sentimental acting.

ROLES IN CONTEMPORARY PLAYS

Thirty-eight of Garrick's roles, the largest number from any
period of dramatic literature on which he had to draw, came in
plays composed between 1737 and 1765, when Garrick ceased
to add new speaking roles to his repertoire. His thirty-ninth new
part came not from a play, but rather from a pageant of Shakespearian characters which Garrick produced for the belated
Shakespeare bicentennial at Stratford in 1769 and then later
adapted for production at Drury Lane. Eight of his roles in new
plays, discounting the pageant, came in five of his own comic
afterpieces, and we shall examine this group later for the light
it sheds both on Garrick's acting and on his instinct for public
relations.[22]

Fully half of his thirty-eight speaking roles in contemporary
plays came in blank-verse tragedies and histories.[23] These plays
make up a singularly undistinguished lot, and most of them did
not survive beyond a single season on the stage. As a group,
however, the plays serve to demonstrate the traditional flavor
of much of eighteenth-century dramaturgy. Written to be played
in declamatory style, and modified little in this respect from
tragedy of the late- and post-Restoration, the profile of the heroes in these plays was inherited more or less directly from the
models offered by Otway, Southerne, and Rowe. The heroes of

serious plays contemporary with Garrick's own career tended to be driven by one of two motives, and often by both: the struggle between familial or romantic love and the demands of state; or the plotting to replace a tyrannical or usurping ruler with a rightful displaced heir. All of the characters in this group of plays speak in verse, and the leading ones—those which Garrick took on, generally—are drawn from the highest ranks of society. All the plays, furthermore, are set in royal courts, and many are fixed in foreign or exotic locales. Bearing these features in mind, it becomes apparent that the serious drama written during Garrick's career borrowed many of its leading characteristics from the neoclassical and heroic tragedy of the previous century, and that its traditional components could be accommodated with eighteenth-century sentimentalism. To protagonists of obsession and pride were added a bit of breast-beating, a sudden reformation, or a reconciliation scene, and the figures were effectively updated and given contemporary reference.

Therefore, although his roles in new plays formed the largest single group within his repertoire, the half of them that were tragic, at least, maintained a clearly traditional cast as well. Not only were the newer plays in which he acted influenced by older dramatic models, but his repertoire was also rather heavily weighted toward roles from "old" plays. Thirty-five of his ninety-six roles came in plays written before 1700, and fifty-three of them fell in plays written before the actor's birth in 1717. Of Garrick's twenty most frequently *performed* roles, only three came in new plays. Five of the others among this most popular group came in Shakespearian tragedy, four more in Elizabethan and Jacobean comedy, three—Archer, Sir John Brute, and Don Felix—in post-Restoration comedy, two in the benevolized and moralized post-Restoration tragedy, and one each in Restoration comedy, late Restoration tragedy, and Early Georgian tragedy.[24] Besides suggesting Garrick's preoccupation with the sentimental possibilities of the plays he acted, this profile also indicates his effort as manager to uphold a balanced repertory as his audience seems to have expected him to do. He produced and acted often in new plays, but some of his most distinguished acting came in older ones. Only rarely were his acting and his management, together, sufficient to sustain new works for long before London audiences. And judging from the profile offered by Garrick's most frequently performed roles, that audience preferred more traditional fare.

THE TRADITIONAL AND THE SENTIMENTAL

It was precisely this traditional cast to his repertoire that set Garrick's interpretive tendencies as an actor in such sharp relief. He succeeded often at recreating old heroes in ways which impressed his audience with their easy manner, their continually stated acknowledgment of the primacy of domestic experience, and their sympathetic qualities. Audiences were even more struck by his departures from traditional characterizations, because these characterizations had grown so familiar with their repeated playing in the theaters royal, in some instances for generations before Garrick's debut. New plays took his acting for granted, in a sense, in their incorporation of sentimental motives; older plays absorbed his contributions in ways at times much more striking and original—even when they were not necessarily superior works.

Another reason for Garrick's particular fondness for characters in older plays may owe to his facility as an adaptor. The liberties which he took with older works, and most notoriously with Shakespeare's, often left the plays better suited than were newer ones to the peculiar demands of eighteenth-century taste, and to the strengths of his own acting. Shakespeare's tragedies, after all, maintain a clear residuum of dynamic action to complement the eighteenth-century fondness for sentimental expression; the same cannot be said of the generally static and turgid plays produced by Garrick's contemporaries among the tragic playwrights. Perhaps the difficulty of infusing contemporary tragedy with the same vitality embodied in Shakespeare's work can help to explain why all of Garrick's own original plays were comedies.

In any event, it is clear that his audience preferred the adapted versions of Garrick's *Hamlet*, *King Lear*, and *Macbeth* to a host of plays by contemporary writers. And in this case, at least, our judgment must commend that of Garrick's contemporaries. His success in sustaining and expanding Shakespeare's popularity, together with his ability to support a modified version of neo-classical tragedy on the stage, testifies to the adaptability and immediacy of his acting. His ability to vivify older works owed largely to his recasting of traditional characters as sympathetic and sentimental men. Heroic action was thus removed from its earlier, more exclusive exercises on battlefields and in beds toward more broadly socialized and utilitarian contexts within marriage, within parenthood, and within the family.

NOTES

1. Plays from this period were almost invariably performed in heavily adapted forms on eighteenth-century stages.

2. *The London Stage 1729–1747*, part 3, ed. Arthur H. Scouten (Carbondale: Southern Illinois University Press, 1961), p. 1047.

3. In his 1766 adaptation, Garrick also changed Horner's name to "Belville" and Margery's name to "Miss Peggy," and he rearranged the exposition of the original version so that Peggy is only *engaged* to marry her guardian, the irascible old Moody. Garrick made these changes with an eye to removing the taint of adultery from the principals; and not surprisingly, he left the way open at the end of his own version for the young lovers to marry—another significant change from the original.

4. Robert D. Hume, *The Development of English Drama in the Late Seventeenth Century* (Oxford: The Clarendon Press, 1976), pp. 9, 396–406.

5. According to Robert Gale Noyes in *The Neglected Muse: Restoration and English Tragedy in the Novel (1740–1780)* (Providence: Brown University Press, 1958), p. 21, only Dryden's *Aureng-Zebe* among the heroic tragedies was performed during Garrick's career.

6. Alvin Kernan, *The Cankered Muse* (New Haven: Yale University Press, 1959), pp. 11, 20, 250–52.

7. See Jean B. Kern, *Dramatic Satire in the Age of Walpole, 1720–1750* (Ames: Iowa State University Press, 1976), pp. 93–95.

8. Benedick was one of four roles which Garrick performed more than one hundred times during his career, and it is further notable for its appearance at least once every year in Garrick's seasonal repertoire between 1748–49, when he first played it, and 1775–76, when he retired. For more elaborate statistical breakdowns of Garrick's roles, see the appendixes of George Winchester Stone, Jr., and George M. Kahrl, *David Garrick: A Critical Biography* (Carbondale: Southern Illinois Uni-

versity Press, 1979), and the appendixes of Leigh Woods, "David Garrick and the Actor's Means: A Revolution in Acting-Style, in Relation to the Life of the Times" (Ph.D. dissertation, University of California, Berkeley, 1979).

9. Garrick also retitled *The Winter's Tale*, to read *Florizel and Perdita*, thus stressing the regenerative and romantic parts of the original play.

10. See George Winchester Stone, Jr., "*Romeo and Juliet*: The Source of its Modern Stage Career," *Shakespeare Quarterly*, XV (1964), 194–95.

11. Joseph Donohue, *Dramatic Character in the English Romantic Age* (Princeton: Princeton University Press, 1970), pp. 16–28.

12. Donohue, *Dramatic Character*, p. 27.

13. Harry William Pedicord, *The Theatrical Public in the Time of Garrick* (Carbondale: Southern Illinois University Press, 1966), pp. 68–87.

14. Pedicord, *Theatrical Public*, pp. 94–106.

15. Hannah More, *Memoirs and Correspondence* (1834); cited in Gamini Salgado, *Eyewitnesses of Shakespeare: First Hand Accounts of Performances, 1590–1890* (London: Sussex University Press, 1975), p. 240.

16. For examples, see Thomas Davies, *Dramatic Miscellanies* (London: Printed for the Author, 1784), II, 292, 317–18; and "Examen of the New Comedy, Called the Suspicious Husband" (London, 1747), p. 31. For a more lengthy treatment of the sentimental and domestic motives in Garrick's characterization of King Lear, see Leigh Woods, "Crowns of Straw on Little Men: Garrick's New Heroes," *Shakespeare Quarterly*, 32 (1981), 69–79.

17. Garrick's post-Restoration "reformed heroes" include:

1. Jealous heroes—Don Carlos in Vanbrugh's *The Mistake*; Don Felix in Susannah Centlivre's *The Wonder*

2. Bullies—Sir John Brute in Vanbrugh's *The Provoked Wife*; Sir Harry Wildair in Farquhar's *The Constant Couple*

3. Rakes—Loveless in Cibber's *Love's Last Shift*; Sir Harry Wildair, Captain Plume in Farquhar's *The Recruiting Officer*.

Although he acknowledges a general pattern of softening in the drawing of the rake-figure which extends through the late- and post-Restoration periods, Robert D. Hume in "The Myth of the Rake in 'Restoration' Comedy," *Studies in Restoration and Eighteenth-Century Drama*, 10 (1977), 25–55, argues that favorable treatments of rakes constituted only a minority approach to the character even at the height of the Restoration. Reformative treatments of the rake-figure were written even during Garrick's career, and this argues either that rakes were being used to symbolize a dead or dying social order, or that they still claimed contemporary referents in the society of Garrick's time.

18. Garrick's roles as "types" in post-Restoration plays include:

1. Comic servants—Scrub in Farquhar's *The Beaux' Stratagem*; Archer in *The Beaux' Stratagem* (who stands as a leading character in the play and who, significantly, is only pretending to be a servant)
2. Cuckold—Fondlewife in Congreve's *The Old Batchelor*
3. Dullard—Costar Pearmain in Farquhar's *The Recruiting Officer*
4. Petty tyrants—Sir Harry Gubbin in Steele's *The Tender Husband*; Captain Brazen in Farquhar's *The Recruiting Officer*
5. Fops—Clodio in Cibber's *Love Makes a Man*; Witwoud in Congreve's *The Way of the World*; Duretete in Farquhar's *The Inconstant*; Lord Foppington in Cibber's *The Careless Husband*; Marplot in Centlivre's *The Busy Body*.

19. Francis Gentleman, *The Dramatic Censor* (London: Printed for J. Bell, 1770), I, 51–52.

20. Hume, *Development of English Drama*, p. 493.

21. Garrick performed Archer 102 times over 28 seasons; Sir John Brute 104 times over 30 seasons; and Don Felix 70 times over 15 seasons. My figures for the total number of Garrick's performances in many roles and per season differ slightly from those published in Appendixes B and C of Stone and Kahrl, *David Garrick*. Stone and Kahrl's figures were gathered from Ben Ross Schneider, Jr., *Index to the London Stage, 1660–1800* (Carbondale: Southern Illinois University Press, 1979) (computerized), and mine were done by hand from the appropriate volumes of *The London Stage*. The disparities seem to owe to Schneider's entries of only the *first* performance of a role which Garrick gave in a season in his index under "Garrick," and to Schneider's inclusion of any other random mentions of the actor mixed in with performance dates. Appendix G of Woods, "David Garrick and the Actor's Means," pp. 399–459, includes breakdowns by date and role for each of the seasons in which Garrick acted and so can be checked for accuracy against *The London Stage*.

22. Garrick's roles in his own plays include Sharp in *The Lying Valet*; the Poet, Frenchman, Drunken Man, and, in post–1756 versions, Lord Chalkstone in *Lethe*; Fribble in *Miss in Her Teens*; Heartly in *The Guardian*; and the Farmer in *The Farmer's Return from London*.

23. Garrick's roles in contemporary blank-verse tragedies include

1. Alfred in *Alfred, A Masque* by David Mallet and James Thomson
2. Regulus in *Regulus* by William Havard

3. Zaphna in *Mahomet* by J. Miller and J. Hoadly

4. Tancred in *Tancred and Sigismunda* by James Thomson

5. Demetrius in *Irene* by Samuel Johnson

6. Eumenes/Dorilas in *Merope* by Aaron Hill

7. Edward in *Edward the Black Prince* by William Shirley

8. Horatius in *The Roman Father* by William Whitehead

9. Mercour in *Eugenia* by Philip Francis

10. Demetrius in *The Brothers* by Edward Young

11. Dumnorix in *Boadicea* by Richard Glover

12. Virginius in *Virginia* by Henry Crisp

13. Aletes/Nicander in *Creusa* by William Whitehead

14. Achmet in *Barbarossa* by John Brown

15. Athelstan in *Athelstan* by John Brown

16. Lysander in *Agis* by John Home

17. Zamti in *The Orphan of China* by Arthur Murphy

18. Aemilius in *The Siege of Aquileia* by John Home

19. Don Alonzo in *Elvira* by David Mallet.

24. Garrick's twenty most frequently performed roles, broken down according to dramatic period and type, are:

Shakespearian tragedy: King Lear, Hamlet, Richard III, Romeo, Macbeth

Elizabethan and Jacobean comedy: Benedick in *Much Ado About Nothing*; Abel Drugger in Jonson's *The Alchemist;* Kitely in Jonson's *Every Man in His Humour*; Leon in Fletcher's *Rule a Wife and Have a Wife*

Contemporary plays: Ranger in Benjamin Hoadly's *The Suspicious Husband*; Lord Chalkstone in Garrick's *Lethe*, Fribble in Garrick's *Miss in Her Teens*

Post-Restoration comedy: Sir John Brute in Vanbrugh's *The Provoked Wife*; Archer in Farquhar's *The Beaux' Stratagem*; Don Felix in Susannah Centlivre's *The Wonder*

Post-Restoration tragedy: Lothario in Rowe's *The Fair Penitent*; Hastings in Rowe's *Jane Shore*

Restoration comedy: Bayes in George Villiers, the Duke of Buckingham's *The Rehearsal*

(Late) Restoration tragedy: Chamont in Otway's *The Orphan*

Early Georgian tragedy: Lusignan in Aaron Hill's *Zara*.

Garrick as Don John in *The Chances,* from a painting by P. J. de Louth-
erbourg. Crown Copyright Victoria and Albert Museum (Theatre Museum).

4

The Actor and the Child

The longevity and intensity of Garrick's popularity on the stage are not entirely attributable to the shape of his repertoire or the originality of his acting. There was something in the man which craved the attention of all sorts of people, in virtually any setting, and this aroused suspicion and, at times, resentment among even his closest friends. Retaliating to Garrick's mock epitaph for him,—"Here lies Nolly Goldsmith, for shortness call'd Noll / Who wrote like an angel, but talk'd like poor Poll!"[1]— Oliver Goldsmith rejoined rather sharply and at some length;

> Here lies David Garrick, describe me who can,
> An abridgment of all that was pleasant in man;
> As an actor, confess'd without rival to shine;
> As a wit, if not first, in the very first line;
> Yet with talents like these, and an excellent heart,
> The man had his failings. A dupe to his art,
> Like an ill-judging beauty, his colours he spread,
> And beplastered with rouge, his own natural red.
> On the stage, he was natural, simple, affecting;
> 'Twas only that when he was off, he was acting.
> With no reason on earth to go out of his way,
> He turn'd and he varied, full ten times a day.
> Though secure of our hearts, though confoundedly sick
> If they were not his own by finessing or trick,
> He cast off his friends as a huntsman his pack

> For he knew when he pleased he could whistle them back.
> Of praise a mere glutton, he swallowed what came,
> And the puff of a dunce, he mistook it for fame,
> Till, his relish grown callous, almost to disease,
> Who pepper'd the highest, was surest to please. . . . [2]

This chapter examines Garrick's background and personality in some detail, the manner in which these influenced his choice of the stage as his career, and the reasons why these sometimes aroused suspicion and animosity.

GARRICK UNDER FIRE

The reservations Garrick's extraordinary animation and garrulity aroused had first been stated by Horace Walpole, whose tastes and manners may have predisposed him to dislike the actor. But similar reservations were voiced by several of Garrick's most prominent and influential friends, all of whom sounded variations on a few consistent themes: that Garrick could be superficial and manipulative in his dealings with others, undiscriminating in his pursuit of praise, and calculating in his choice and cultivation of friends.

In a 1752 edition of *The Rambler*, Samuel Johnson wrote what many of his contemporaries interpreted as an allegorical treatment of his relationship to Garrick.[3] In it, Johnson referred to himself as "Asper" and to Garrick, perhaps, as "Prospero," and he described a situation in which the two old friends meet after Prospero has achieved great wealth. Throughout the story, Prospero alternates between ostentation and patronization as he guides Asper through his well-appointed house. Although it becomes obvious to Prospero that Asper is leading a struggling existence, even as Johnson was during many of the years in which Garrick flourished, Prospero makes no offer to aid him and he withholds from Asper several amenities, including his best china and his finest tea.

If this piece is indeed a literal treatment of Johnson's view of the relationship between himself and Garrick, it seems odd that Johnson's only reference to Garrick's profession—the source of all the actor's considerable wealth—should have come in the choice of the name "Prospero," a role which Garrick never played. Known to have little respect for acting, Johnson simply may not have deigned to mention it, or not ascribed to it any role in Garrick's faults as a man. On another occasion Johnson would compare an actor's function to that of a "rope-dancer, or a ballad singer."[4] In Johnson's mind, the implications of being an actor were not evil, apparently, but merely frivolous, and the rewards which attached to the practice of the acting profession at its highest levels disproportionate to the point of obscenity.

To some extent, too, Garrick seems always to have remained the student in Johnson's mind, and the actor fed this habit by his generally deferential manner toward his former teacher. The older man often pinpointed the source of Garrick's enormous popular success dismissively in the actor's boyhood facility as a mimic; and in this connection Johnson seems to have shared Walpole's deprecating attitude toward the function of mimicry in acting, and with it something of the bias against an activity regarded as "imitative" by nature, rather than as generative or truly inventive.

Like Walpole, and Macklin too, Johnson was skeptical of the authenticity of the emotion which Garrick expressed on the stage. When David once chastened Johnson for talking too loudly backstage and destroying feelings necessary to the character he was playing that night, Johnson had only replied, "Pshaw, sir— Punch has no feelings!"[5] In Johnson's mention of Punch, the English version of a clown derived from the *commedia dell'arte*, there reappears the association of acting with clowning invoked by Theophilus Cibber and Horace Walpole. Such associations worked always to equate Garrick, in his physical slightness, his restless animation, his "pert vivacity," and his pandering to the tastes of the ignorant, with the coarseness and debasement of the clowns from the public fairgrounds.

Garrick seems to have gone to some pains early in his career to acquire accomplishments which would stamp him as a gentleman, and so remove his acting from the accusations of vulgarity which sprinkled the early criticism of it. Benjamin Victor, in his brief biographical sketch of the actor which introduced Garrick's collection of *Dramatic Works* (1774), wrote that "having added the qualifications of dancing and fencing, to that natural gentility of manner, which no art can bestow . . . his deportment is constantly easy, natural, and engaging."[6] Even before his debut as an actor Garrick mounted a literary career, and he sustained it during the busiest years of his life as something which could stand as a more refined and broadly respectable complement to his acting. It is interesting, too, that Victor's testimony to Garrick's genteel accomplishments should have fallen in a collection of the actor's literary works, in the place where it was most likely to be credited by those who may have been reluctant still to do so otherwise.

Samuel Johnson's notion that "Garrick's trade was to represent passion, not to feel it" further illustrates the classical attitude toward acting as a craft or "trade" which lacked the standing of the professions or of the authentic compositional arts.[7] Johnson's definition of "drama" in his *A Dictionary of the English Language* (1775) as "a poem accommodated to action" indicates the firmness of his belief, shared by others with his erudition and classical background, that the practical arts of the stage were derivative from and subordinate to the germinative activity of the playwright-poet.

The images Johnson used to describe Garrick's acting were drawn, not surprisingly, from Johnson's own discipline of writing. To Joshua Reynolds he claimed that Garrick's "every gesture . . . was settled in his closet before he set foot upon the stage."[8] He may have been right in this: We shall look at evidences of Garrick's meticulous planning as an actor and as a manager in the next chapter. But Garrick himself claimed that an actor was not a true genius without "those instantaneous feelings, that Life blood, that keen Sensibility, that bursts at once from Genius, and like Electrical fire shoots thro' the Veins, Marrow, and Bones and all, of every Spectator."[9] In this passage, quoted frequently since as one of Garrick's few pronouncements about acting as a discrete art, he affirms the importance of spontaneous impulse to any actor who would claim distinction, and he argues, by implication, that such a gift removes the actor who possesses it from being categorized as a mere imitator.

Standing not more than five feet, four inches tall and quite slender at the beginning of his career, Garrick's lightness and compactness marked him off from the generally larger and more heavyset English tragic actors who had taken leading roles before him. So, too, did his agility, and George Lichtenberg described the quality of Garrick's movement as Abel Drugger when the actor was in his late fifties and near the end of his career: ". . . He boxes, he runs about and skips from one neat leg to the other with such admirable lightness that one would dare swear he was floating in the air."[10] It was precisely this nimbleness—and his lack of size and of sheer muscular power—which encouraged Garrick at the beginning of his career to perfect an acting style which would stress grace and rapidity of movement rather than statuesque dignity. It also happened that his own physical qualities and the style to which they contributed accorded well with the taste of his age for a more subtle and refined physical expressiveness—the "feeling" part of sentiment. What emerged in Garrick, fostered both by his own inclinations and by his audience's preference, was a "sensitive" style in its responsiveness to the slightest details of physical environment, as well as in its admission of a broader range of human emotions than had been used by earlier actors. It was not that a larger and heavier actor could not have done this, but that a smaller and lighter one *had* to, and that most of his audience applauded him for it.

Garrick's initially slender physical frame was joined to a life-long disposition toward colds and respiratory congestion,[11] and the combination created a speaking voice which, according to fellow-actor Thomas Davies, "wanted that fulness of sound, that *os rotundum*, to roll with ease a long declamatory speech, or give force and dignity to mere sentiment."[12] According to Lucille S. Rubin, although Garrick's voice was flexible and mutable, he "did not possess a powerful stage voice. Frequently he could not depend on his voice, and at times he was literally without it."[13] Indeed, the story was handed down that Garrick had made it through his debut only with help from a juicy orange which someone handed him backstage when his voice began to flag in the middle of his Richard III.[14]

Davies resurrected after Garrick's death the criticisms of the actor's lack of physical size and vocal power when tested against booming, martial roles. Particularly when Garrick was paired with more vocally formidable actors, the disparity between him and the others onstage could be telling, as when he played Hotspur opposite the Falstaff of James Quin: "The person of Garrick was not formed to give a just idea of the gallant and noble Hotspur. The mechanic, or bulky, part was wanting; nor could the fine flexibility of his voice entirely conquer the high rant and continued rage of the enthusiastic warrior."[15] In such accounts, Garrick's attempt to enlarge himself onstage is almost palpable, and it worked, at times, to make him seem ridiculous. When late in his career he recalled his performance as Antony in *Antony and Cleopatra*, he took pride in the fact that the play "gain'd ground Every time it was play'd," but he mentions also that he "grew tir'd, & gave it up."[16] Presumably, he found exhausting the physical requirements of a role largely defined in martial actions, or at least in references to such, and in larger-than-life passions. As Othello, the problem of his size seems to have been aggravated by a makeup which obscured his expressive face, and by a particularly unflattering costume. Quin, who had played the role himself and was hungry for vindication of his own acting, ridiculed Garrick in the role by comparing him to a Negro slave-boy in one of Hogarth's paintings from "The Harlot's Progress": "Here's Pompey!" crowed Quin to Dr. Hoadly as they sat together in the theater, "but where's the teakettle and lamp?"[17]

The same gifts of quickness, lightness, and flexibility which served him so well in sentimental roles and which qualified him for both tragedy and comedy were ill-adapted to the heavier kinds of heroes in the repertory, roles which demanded either an imposing physique, a powerful voice, a prepotent dignity, or the continual reiteration of the same passion. Such roles gave Garrick little scope for what were his distinctive expressive strengths, and the ways he found to play these roles contributed much to the general softening of the figure of the neoclassical paragon on eighteenth-century stages, even if they were not always popular or critical successes.

ALMOST GROWING UP

Quin's criticism of Garrick's Othello for its being childlike suggests another avenue of exploration. The actor's smallness, his playfulness, his imaginative freedom, and his characteristic self-deprecation raise the question of the degree to which the pleasure which Garrick found in acting owed to influences from his early life. Is it possible to trace the sources of Garrick's animation, and of the calculation that sometimes went with it, to his experience before he became an actor?

If it is not, we have none other than Samuel Johnson to blame for tempting us that way. When Davies solicited Johnson for information about the young Garrick in the year following the actor's death, Johnson recalled David as "a most sprightly and diverting boy" who had as a child "engaged the attention of every body who knew him."[18] Garrick succeeded not only in gaining Johnson's attention, but also that of Gilbert Walmesley, Registrar of the Ecclesiastical Court of Lichfield and one of the most important men in the town. When David's father was stationed abroad on an army commission, Walmesley seems to have appointed himself a sort of surrogate father for the boy, first assuming responsibility for his education and later, when the young man was ready to try his fortune in London, writing him a letter of recommendation to one of Walmesley's oldest clerical friends there. In the letter, Walmesley asked the Reverend Mr. Colson to board and instruct the nineteen-year-old Garrick as a prospective law student, and Walmesley vouched for him as "of sober and good dispositions, and . . . as ingenious and promising a young man as ever I knew in my life."[19] Walmesley may have described Garrick as "sober," but it is likely that something in David's personality, and his ability to repeat passages from current plays and satires, appealed to the unmarried, middle-aged man.[20] Walmesley certainly knew young Garrick well by the time he wrote the recommendation to Colson that "this young gentleman . . . has been much with me, ever since he was a child, almost every day; and I have taken a pleasure often in instructing him."[21]

Once in London, David tried to enter a serious profession, first the law, a short-lived experiment, and afterward the wine trade, in partnership with his older brother Peter. Always a bright and promising boy, David's family may have expected impressive achievements from him. His correspondence with his father suggests that Captain Garrick, while absent in Gibraltar, was counting on David's attending a university, although David protested that his trip abroad several years earlier had "backened" him in his schoolwork.[22] Somewhere between the ages of eight and fifteen, David was sent by his parents to Portugal to live with his rich uncle, also named David Garrick, who was a wine merchant in Lisbon. The experiment seems to have been intended to draw some of the uncle's money toward a struggling family, to assist him in the conduct of his own business, and to serve as an apprenticeship of sorts for the young nephew. Although David had stayed only a year, he later entered the wine business with the legacy his uncle willed him; and given Garrick's later success as an adult at charming the rich and the famous, it is striking that he should have accomplished this feat twice by the time he was nineteen, the first time with his uncle and the second with Gilbert Walmesley.

As a young boy in a foreign land, Garrick made his mark on the small English merchant community in the way that later became the professional extension of his adult life. Describing the entertainments of the Lisbon-based merchants, Davies reports that "after dinner they usually diverted themselves by placing him [David] upon the table, and calling upon him to repeat verses and speeches from plays, which he did with great readiness, and much to the satisfaction of the hearers. Some Portuguese young gentlemen of the highest rank, who were of his own age, were also much delighted with his conversation."[23] Garrick's precocious interest in performing reappears a bit later when, having returned home and with his older brother, Peter, gone to sea, David assumed responsibility for writing family letters to his father, who in the early- and mid-1730s was stationed on Gibraltar. Eleven of these letters written by David between the ages of fifteen and eighteen have survived. In them Garrick refers once to the character of Captain Brazen, when he quotes to his father a line from Farquhar's *The Recruiting Officer*, and once to a local "Halequin" [*sic*] who has composed a political satire which David sends along for his father's amusement.[24] Three from among this set of letters include excerpts from satires which David remembered and set down.[25] His youthful awareness of the theater is further documented by his description to his father of a royal wedding. In it David showed some aptitude for recalling and arranging atmospheric detail, anticipating his later scenic and materialist awareness as an actor: "We have had great rejoicings all over England, on account of the Nuptials of ye Prince of Orange with ye Princess Royall, every Body almost wears Orange Cockades & favours, houses are illuminated, Burnfires, Drinking ye health of ye Royal couple. . . ."[26]

When Joshua Reynolds described Garrick more than a decade after the actor's death, he attributed the intensity of Garrick's need for attention to his formative experience: "Garrick, from his early youth, when he used to repeat passages in plays and act whole parts in private theatres, naturally imbibed a desire for popular applause. Afterwards, when he entered the great world and had enlarged his circle, this universal passion was not likely to be much abated; 'twas the employment of his mind, night and day, by what means he could improve and advance his reputation."[27] Reynolds may have overstated the compulsive nature of Garrick's pursuit of reputation, but his tracing of Garrick's fondness for attention back to the actor's childhood does not seem far-fetched. Davies reported that Garrick's first performance had come as "Serjeant Kite" in a production of *The Recruiting Officer* which David himself cast and staged with some of his siblings and with other children from Lichfield.[28] About eleven at the time, Garrick may have chosen his role as a soldier, his subordinate rank, and a play about soldiers set in a small provincial town in deference to his father who was himself a recruiting officer as long as he was stationed in Lichfield. The production seems to have engraved itself on David's memory, for as we have seen, he was to quote a line from the play to his father, absent in Gibraltar, several years later.

This story also provides an early instance of Garrick's artistic tendency to draw on his own immediate experience in his sympathetic approach to dramatic character, and it offers a practical instance of the naturalistic component of his acting which so struck audience members and critics on the night of his London debut as Richard III. Far from criticizing reality as he saw it, Garrick seems rather to have prized it and to have used it as a base for idealizing. During his professional career he was to play three more roles from *The Recruiting Officer*: Costar Pearmain, the dull recruit; Captain Brazen, the loud, ineffectual braggart; and Captain Plume, the handsome young officer who tumbles a few of the local ladies and is "reformed," finally, by the young woman he comes to love. It is notable that in the two latter roles, which he played most often, he "promoted" himself to his father's terminal rank. In no other single play did Garrick take more than two roles.

Furthermore, a rough count shows that about thirty of Garrick's ninety-six professional roles came as soldiers of various descriptions.[29] This fact may suggest as much about the flavor of contemporary repertories, still imbued in the remnants of traditional models of heroism, as it does about Garrick's desire to recreate portions of his father's experience on the stage. On the other hand, in 1745, having already established himself as England's leading actor, Garrick volunteered to serve under Lord Rochester in the force which that peer was mustering to repel the invading army of "Bonny Prince Charlie."[30] His offer was refused, politely but firmly, and Garrick traveled instead to act in Dublin. But his attempt to enlist seems to have been made in good faith, and even with his father eight years dead, Garrick may still have been interested in emulating him, after a fashion. His interest in acting seems never to have represented a rebellion against his family's values or a renunciation of his own background; and as we have seen, nearly one-third of his life as an actor was to be spent in imaginative recreation of the circumstances of his father's respectable, impecunious, and often isolating profession.

Feeling sympathetic to his father after the captain's death may have been especially important to David, in the degree that sympathy may not always have existed between the two during the father's life.[31] From David's earliest preserved letters, it is clear that Captain Garrick's absence in Gibraltar put a great strain on the Garrick family generally, and on David in particular by elevating him while still in his early- or mid-teens to a standing at the head of his family. At least once his father taxed him with being dilatory in his responsibility for writing family news down and sending it off to Gibraltar, and David defended himself against this charge in a lengthy protestation which takes up the major part of one entire letter:

. . . It would be the worst of ingratitude, and I ought to be esteem'd
ye worst of Wretches, did I neglect, what I thought would give ye least
pleasure and Satisfaction to one of the best of Fathers. If those Persons who have not in any measure receiv'd what tenderness & Affection, I have, from their Parents, are accounted Reprobates, if they om-
itt [*sic*] to pay all ye Regard and obedience to them they possibly can,
what on ye contrary can be said for him who in every instance of Life,
has had ye greatest indulgences from a most kind father, whose study
has always been to promote the welfare of his Children, such a one I
think that does not return Paternal love with filial affection is ye most
odious Monster, and rather fit for ye Society of Brutes than that of
Men. . . .[32]

The seventeen-year-old David's writing savors here of the formal, the conventional, and the theatrical, and it is interesting
that the issue of "filial affection" would later lie at the heart of
two of his most famous characterizations—as Hamlet and King
Lear. About a year after this effusion, David defended himself
again, though this time with rather more humor: "If the Sea
was as sure to carry, As I am to write, you would have no reason to complain of my Neglect, or a Son's Disobedience."[33]

Mrs. Garrick's health was not good during much of this five-
year period of the captain's absence, and David dutifully passed
along her succession of illnesses (some of which seem psycho-
somatic in nature) to his father. And there seem to have been
other strains. In 1773 Garrick reportedly told Percival Stockdale that when his father had finally returned home, David
greeted him with a curious interrogatory: " 'I suppose, sir . . .
I have a good many brothers and sisters, at Gibraltar?' Tears
came into the eyes of poor Mrs. Garrick. 'Hold your tongue,
Davy;' (said the captain) 'Don't talk in that manner; you see how
it affects your mother.' 'I was then,' (continued Garrick to me)
'a thoughtless little boy; I would not for the world have wounded
my mother's feelings; I only fancied that I had hit upon an excellent joke.' "[34] If the story is true (and there are certainly some
errors, at least in Stockdale's telling of it), it is noteworthy that
the captain did not trouble to deny his son's charge, and that
David's concern in the incident was entirely for his mother's
feelings. Captain Garrick died in 1737, less than a year after his

return to Lichfield, and Garrick left for London with Samuel Johnson on March 2 of that year, exactly seventeen days before his father's passing.[35] His departure may have been dictated by financial necessity, particularly if his father's illness was lingering, a possibility which is suggested by Captain Garrick's signing of a will on January 1, 1737.[36] If nothing else, David's sense of timing in this instance, always so good onstage once he became an actor, let him down. David's father left him only £1 out of £2,500, although this may have had to do with the £1,000 legacy which David had received from his uncle and namesake in the year previous.[37]

Garrick's small size, his quick and at times sharp wit, and his gifts as a social creature in all companies may have appealed more to other members of his family than they did to his father. J. H. Plumb has discussed the general tendency of a "social" education to replace a more traditional religious one during the eighteenth century, and he has speculated that the beginnings of a published literature for juveniles indicates that children were accorded greater status and attention than had been the case before among middle-class families.[38] Evidence about the details of David's upbringing is scant, but with his father in the army enjoying the traditional male fellowship which that institution afforded, David must have seen more of his mother and perhaps been more influenced by her while he was growing up. If we add this probability to Lawrence Stone's image of the "child-oriented, affectionate and permissive" child rearing which gained currency among middle-class families during the eighteenth century, we may begin to understand the kind of encouragement Garrick got as a child toward the expressive freedom, confidence, and sympathy he manifested as an adult, both on the stage and away from it.[39]

Garrick seems always to have loved attention—and lots of it—and he preferred even ridicule to indifference, as we shall see a bit later. He may have been used to a good deal of attention from his premature standing as man of the house while still in adolescence, with his father away from home, and even earlier, perhaps, as boy of the house with his cleverness and charm. The presence of affection in his family seems clear enough in its frequent and spontaneous expressions throughout Garrick's correspondence; but if this affection was indeed selective while his parents were living, as it was almost certain to be, at times, in a family of seven children, Garrick may have grown skilled at an early age in attracting attention both from and within crowds. Playfulness lingered on conspicuously in his adult behavior, and we can only wonder at the extent to which its early appearances had been calculated to draw all eyes to himself— and at who, besides Gilbert Walmesley, the Lisbon merchants, and the Lichfield gathering at Garrick's youthful production of *The Recruiting Officer*, had inspired in young David a taste for the attention of the greater world.

CHILDHOOD EXTENDED, IN A MOSTLY INDULGENT WORLD

When as a child he cast his production of *The Recruiting Officer*, Garrick chose for himself neither the lead (the dashing Captain Plume) nor the richest comic role (the braggart-warrior Captain Brazen), both of which he would play later as a professional. In Sergeant Kite, rather, Garrick selected a supporting role, but one which works to unify the play and to join, in its contact with most of the other charaters, the play's several subplots. It is Kite who of all the characters comes closest to being the "engine" of the play. In this case, Garrick's willingness to accept responsibility for the entire production seems to have prevailed over his desire to feature himself, both in his choice of role and in his function as the managing and producing agent.

This inclination is especially significant appearing, as it did, in a situation which Garrick seems to have been able to influence and control in a number of ways. Such a model was one which would be re-created when Garrick succeeded to the managership of the Drury Lane company, a position he then held from 1747 until his retirement in 1776, with only two years off while he traveled in Europe. His ideals of fame and praise required the admiration not only of his audience, it seems, but also of his coworkers and collaborators; and the theater seems to have served Garrick's need for social and communal experience in some of the same ways that his family had.

We have seen already how the model of "sympathy" was one which suggested that feeling and virtue were communicable, either between individuals, from the one to the many, or from the many to the one. In the richness and vitality of its conduct, Garrick's career seems to have bridged all these gaps. His interests both as manager and as actor caused him to stress the critical importance of ensemble playing,[40] and his positive image of the powers of capitalistic enterprise helped him to construct elaborate interdependencies within his ever-growing company at Drury Lane.[41] Creating dependency on himself—as a writer, as a manager, as an administrator, and as a philanthropist—may have represented Garrick's attempt to attract attention in ways he and his society considered more legitimate than performing.

A profile of Garrick emerges, both as a child and as a man, of someone quick, attractive, and conscientious, eager to please and capable of gathering, charming, and entertaining audiences wherever he found the beginnings of them. He seems never to have been given to speculation and introspection. He had a gift of charm, to which all but a few were susceptible, and the natural place for its exercise was in "the great world" of London theater and society. His friends were numerous, and his life, particularly after his retirement from the stage, seems to have been one dizzying social round. He flourished when in the company of others, and he seems to have been most relaxed not when alone, but rather when in the presence of small groups of friends. He once boasted that he had never spent a single night apart from his wife in the time they had been married.[42]

If it is accurate, this profile works to confirm the sense that Garrick's interest in acting was sparked and sustained not by an idealized and refined image of the player's calling, but as an activity in which he could exercise his social acuity, his need for approval, and his desire, perhaps, to re-create the circumstances of his place within his family—admired, flattered, trusted, and applauded. Nor is it surprising, if Joshua Reynolds's hypothesis about the influence of Garrick's early years on his acting is correct, that the actor's talents coalesced so neatly with the demands of the sentimental and domestic plays being written during the course of his career. Garrick may have been extraordinary in his natural gifts, but he was typical of his time in the relation his background forged between his life and his art.

It would also appear that Garrick equated the applause he was able to generate as a performer with his acceptance in "the great world." In his first letter to his older brother following his debut performance in London, Garrick refers to "ye Surprize of Every Body" at his first Richard III,[43] and he would later argue the legitimacy of acting to his brother by claiming the approval of the titled and prominent: "Mr Littleton Mr Pit & Several Other Members of Parliament were to See Me play Chamont in ye Orphan & Mr Pit, who is reckon'd ye Greatest Orator in the house of Commons, said I was best Actor ye English Stage had produced. . . . the Prince of Wales has heard so great a Character of Me that we are in daily Expectations of his comming [sic] to See Me. . . ."[44] In April 1742, Garrick wrote to Peter again about his new friendships with the Lords Hallifax, Sandwich, and Chesterfield, and he concluded his letter with the claim that "I believe nobody (as an Actor) was ever more caress'd & My Character as a private Man makes ['em] more desirous of my Company—(all this Entre nous as one Brothr to Another). . . .";[45] The word *caressed* appears again in a letter Garrick wrote from Dublin during the summer of 1742,[46] when David became the object of what was called at the time "Garrick fever."[47] And from Paris in 1763, he mentions his being "now star'd at [in?] ye Playhouse, & talk'd of by Gentle & Simple as ye most wonderfull Wonder of Wonders."[48]

All of these pleasurable sensations were triggered by the responses of others to his acting, and his repeated use of the word *caressed* suggests that the gratification he received from acting was at least partly physical in its nature. Just as his acting style was based on an expanded use of sensory resources, a heightened awareness of the physical environment, and a total bodily commitment to sentimental material, so did his reward from that acting spring from his sensory apparatus, too. The sort of "feeling" contained in eighteenth-century theatergoing assumed that the actor and his audience were symbiotic entities. As well as describing the functions of genius, then, Garrick was trying to capture the sensory tie between actor and audience when he depicted "that Life blood, that keen Sensibility, that bursts at once from Genius, and like Electrical fire shoots thro' the Veins, Marrow, and Bones and all, of every Spectator." The acts both of impersonation and of playgoing were seen in Garrick's time as rooted in the body; and the intensity of the processes in their mutual reverberations surprised even Garrick at the beginning of his career. His "Entre nous" caution to his brother suggests his amazement that something which seemed easy to him, and so indistinguishable from his natural "Character as a private Man," should bring him attention from such lofty quarters.

The first wave of popular acclaim which followed his debut appears to have served Garrick in the nature of a tonic. After having complained to Peter that his "Illness and lowness of Spirits was owing to my want of resolution to tell You my thoughts" about becoming an actor,[49] three and one-half months later Garrick wrote to his brother that "I never was better in health in my Life & can undergo fatigue like a little Hercules."[50] Garrick's sense of strength and purpose during his first season on the stage is confirmed by his appearance on 136 playing nights (including one on Christmas night), and on 26 of these occasions he followed a role in the mainpiece with one more in the afterpiece.[51]

As much as he enjoyed his fame, Garrick seems often to have looked for ways of sharing his enjoyment with others. His first role, after his wedding to Eva-Maria Veigel in 1749, was the good-natured and finally marriageable Benedick in Shakespeare's *Much Ado about Nothing*.[52] It would also be his first performance on his return to England from his travels on the continent, as a celebration of the fulfillment which he found in his marriage. Percy Fitzgerald describes that marriage in fulsome terms, but the tone of his account is consistent with contemporary descriptions of Garrick's wedded life:

It is remarkable that in the enormous mass of correspondence preserved by Garrick—and he seemed to preserve every scrap that was addressed to him—there is not a single letter of Mrs. Garrick's. The simple reason for this is, that she had no occasion to write to him, as he was literally never absent from her a day. When he went abroad Mrs. Garrick went abroad with him; when he went to the "great houses" on visits, Mrs. Garrick was taken also. She was invited behind the scenes, listened to the rehearsals, and gave her judgment. The economy of the theatre—its accounts—everything was carefully looked to by this ad-

mirable and invaluable lady. There was a charming delicacy and gallantry in his behaviour to her, the bloom of which was never lost.
Nothing was complete in either his business or his pleasure without
her. If a new actor were to exhibit his powers at Southampton Street,
Mrs. Garrick was laughingly put behind a screen to have her share of
the "fun." She had her box at Drury Lane. When Mr. Garrick was
painted again and again by all painters, he was most pleased with those
paintings where she was brought in. There were many husbands who
might pay such attentions; but none could rival the charming delicacy,
and almost loverlike gallantry, which he maintained towards her to the
end.[53]

Thus was the preeminent domestic hero of the eighteenth-century stage a sort of domestic hero in life as well.

Garrick was acutely aware of the effect which he made, both
in life and on the stage, and he was, in this, very much and very
conventionally the actor. His desire seems not to have been to
gain praise by misrepresenting himself, but rather by disposing
his own spontaneous and often generous nature to best advantage. Garrick was fortunate, too, that the leading features of his
personality were so marketable in the society for which he performed. He seems to have made little distinction between his
public function as an actor and his private behavior in many
situations. It may have been the lack of such distinctions which
contributed to his remarkable expressiveness on the stage. It may
also be that the similarity between areas of his onstage and offstage deportment confused and troubled friends like Goldsmith, Reynolds, and Johnson, to whom the elements of calculation in both parts of Garrick's behavior figured more
prominently than did those of consistency and spontaneity.
Perhaps it was the same thing they distrusted that went into
making Garrick an actor in the first place.

Bearing in mind again Reynolds's hypothesis that Garrick's
need for praise originated in his early experience, the prominence of this drive in the actor's adult life may well have lacked
some of the innocence of its formative expressions. Even in its
later forms, however, it seems to have functioned often in an
involuntary and habitual way, rather than in a patently design-
ing one. Many of his contemporaries remarked on Garrick's
impulsiveness, and the frequency of such observations adds

weight to the notion that Garrick's attempts to elicit applause from quarters other than the stage may not always have been premeditated and self-serving. Samuel Johnson, for instance, balanced his criticisms of Garrick to Reynolds by affirming that "As a man he was kind, friendly, benevolent, and generous."[54]

Another factor which argues the reflexive nature of at least some of Garrick's private behavior is his development, over a period of years, of a conversational style characterized by frequent pauses, hesitations, and digressions. Tate Wilkinson, an actor-manager himself and a mimic of some note, re-created Garrick's distinctive speech in his memoirs. On one occasion, when Wilkinson had asked him for the favor of a benefit performance, Garrick supposedly replied:

Why now, that is, why! Hey, Cross, and be damned to you!—Hey, why now, that is—and I really do not see, how that you, young Wilkinson, can be able, that is to say, or for you to presume to pay the expense of a benefit? It now really is, and so does Mrs. Garrick think, an enormous expense; and I do not see—but indeed with a partner I will consent to it—but not otherwise on any account.[55]

Just as John Hill testified that Garrick's habit of pausing as he spoke verse had become "much worse than at first" by 1750,[56] so Thomas Davies described Garrick's distinctive private speech in the later stages of the actor's life: "The quickness of his conceptions, and the precipitance of his temper, obliged him to make use of that caution, which some persons think degenerated into an art. I do not remember, that in the younger part of his life, and before he was a manager, he had any notable hesitation of speech, which afterwards was so universally observed in him."[57]

Davies attributed Garrick's speaking pattern to the actor's need of guarding against the unhappy consequences of his own impulsiveness, and he makes explicit the concern about Garrick's translation of his art into his life which was felt by so many of the actor's acquaintances. The frequency with which this concern was expressed will suggest, if nothing else, that Garrick may not have been so good an actor in his private life as he was on the stage. This appears to have been especially true of Garrick's responses when he was under unusual stress, and we shall look next at several such reactions.

SELF-CONSCIOUSNESS AND APOLOGIZING

Like many prominent people, Garrick seems to have adopted a manner which allowed him to remain noncommittal. It is likely that a certain amount of "managing," in this connection, was necessary simply in order to get him through his busy days at Drury Lane. Once Garrick assumed the patent there, in 1747, he came open to attacks from some new sources, including the ranks of disappointed actors he failed to hire into the company and of playwrights whose works he declined to stage. He was subject at times to political attacks as well, and in 1755, with Britain at the brink of war with France, Garrick engaged a ballet company under Jean Georges Noverre to perform "The Chinese Festival" at his theater. One party among the audience took exception to the presence of "French dancers" in the company, even though most of the dancers with French names were Swiss, like Noverre himself.[58] The run of the piece was disrupted and finally aborted by rioting and the destruction of parts of the theater building.[59] In a similar situation during the 1762–63 season, when Garrick announced an end to the old practice of allowing spectators to enter the theater after the third act of the mainpiece for one-half of the standard admission price, his decision precipitated the aptly named Half Price Riots, which led again to Garrick's capitulation.[60]

When his profits also began to diminish during this troubled 1762–63 season, Garrick's first impulse was to fight in the best way he knew how: His 29 roles that year are the largest number he undertook in a single season, and although his 109 performances are only his third largest total, they came in the forty-seventh year of his life.[61] Never again would Garrick play more than 49 times in a single season. But when all of this activity failed to placate and hold his audience, Garrick withdrew on his Grand Tour of Europe. His departure for Dover and the passage to France came on September 15, 1763, coinciding with the opening performance of that year's season at Drury Lane.[62]

Writing from Paris in 1764, Garrick offered some advice to his hand-picked successor as leading actor in his company, young William Powell. Garrick's tone suggests some of the bitterness he may have felt in the wake of events which he seems to have interpreted as a personal rejection by the London playgoing public:

I have not always met with Gratitude in a play House. . . . Guard against *the Splitting the Ears of the Groundlings who are capable of Nothing but dumb Shew & noise*, [*Hamlet*, III.ii.]—dont sacrifice your taste and ffeelings [*sic*] to the Applause of Multitude; a true Genius will convert an Audience to His Manner, rather than be converted by them to what is false & unnatura[l—] *be not too tame neither*. . . . [III.ii.][63]

A certain pettishness here is more of a piece with the childlike aspect of Garrick's personality than it is with the generally egalitarian and benevolent flavor of his public remarks. It may be, though, that later in his career he began to feel some of the elitism which grew up in Britain as sentimentalism transformed itself into its negative and dangerous corollary, "enthusiasm." Another parallel development associated such enthusiasm with the working class, particularly in its fervor for fundamentalist religions; and the rise of urban ghettos began to mark this class more clearly than before as a distinct and threatening entity.[64] Rioting such as Garrick had witnessed in his own theater in 1763 began to be a more regular and predictable feature of city life, and it seems to have mobilized antidemocratic feelings within the class of urban gentry of which Garrick was a member. In Garrick himself it may have consolidated reservations about the rule of the mob dating back to 1755, when a gang of rioters from "The Chinese Festival" had spilled out of the theater, walked the short distance between the Drury Lane and Garrick's home in Southampton Street, and broken several of his windows.[65] It may be, too, that the old custom of abjection on the part of actors in the face of audience disapproval worked over the long run to fuel some resentment in Garrick. In the aftermath of the Half Price Riots, he had composed a conciliatory "Address to the Town":

Since my good friends, tho' late, are pleas'd at last,
I bear with patience all my suff'rings past;
To you who saw my suff'rings, it is clear,
I bought my secret most confounded dear.
To any gentleman not over nice,

I'll sell 'em all again, and at half price. . . .
There is one secret still remains behind,
Which ever did, and will distract my mind—
I'd give up all for that—nay, fix for ever,
To find the secret—to deserve your favour![66]

One can almost feel Garrick gritting his teeth as he apologized.

His appetite for acting, and for the public who received it, was eventually rekindled by absence and, perhaps, by reports of Powell's resounding success in many of his old roles. Garrick returned to the stage in November 1765, having been away from it for two and one-half years. Scars from the Half Price Riots seem to have remained, though, for some of the ambivalence toward acting evident in his letter to Powell lingered on. In the prologue which he wrote for his return performance, a royal command for Benedick to be played before the king, Garrick asked rhetorically, "Is it not long enough to play the fool?" and a few lines later suggested that he might be "fit for nothing but a Punchinello."[67] This latter remark may offer only an instance of self-pity on Garrick's part, but it is interesting that older views of the actor as buffoon suffused even Garrick's vocabulary on occasion, and that such evaluations had remained familiar enough to him and his audience that England's foremost actor could at least frame them neatly and direct their impact to his own advantage.

Garrick's parading of his ambivalence at performing before an audience which included George III is typical of the actor's life in its mixing of private feeling with public exercise. Just before his return to England, Garrick wrote and had published, anonymously, "The Sick Monkey," a parable in verse about a monkey who is a player in a court composed entirely of other animals. The monkey has fallen sick with an attack of "nerves" when some of the animals have castigated him for his imitations of them. The tone of the piece is light rather than bitter, and it ends with a caution to "Garrick" upon his arrival to ignore groundless criticism and to "Keep the passion from your HEAD, / And clap it to your TAIL."[68]

At the same time that he was derogating his critics, Garrick was suiting his own habit of self-deprecation with his choice of a monkey as the totem for himself. In a later parable which he wrote for a command performance of his play *Lethe*, as a one-man show before the royal family in the year following his retirement, Garrick pictured himself as a blackbird recalled to perform for the other animals at the bidding of an eagle whom the others all respect and obey.[69] It is interesting, first of all, that Garrick should have grouped himself in the same species with the animal-king; but beyond that, we notice that both blackbird and monkey are small and hyperactive creatures, and that each is among the noisiest members of his world. As clowns among animals, too, each is willing to sacrifice dignity in order to compel the attention of his "public." Only by entertaining, in the terms of Garrick's parables, can the blackbird or the monkey assuage, charm, and convert. In these pieces Garrick first anticipated, and later re–created, the flavor of his prodigal prologue in the fall of 1765 before the king, with its belittling images of his own place in society. His consistent desire seems to have been to shrink his physical stature, even as his prestige, social standing, and monopoly over the performing situation grew. Shrinking himself was one thing; but having the audience accept this reduced image was quite another. Garrick grew upset when the royal family did not applaud his *tour de force* in *Lethe* and, apparently discouraged from repeating his disappointment, he did not perform again in the year and one-half of his life which remained.[70]

If he was haunted by the prospect of failure as an actor—and his standard of success was always rather high—the prospect of success as an actor may also have daunted him at the beginning of his career. Gareth Lloyd-Evans has noted Garrick's anonymity in his formal debut in London, when he was featured on handbills to play Richard III only as "a Gentleman (who never appeared on any stage)."[71] On the one hand it was a standard practice to bill newcomers in this way, so as to create the greatest possible sense of anticipation among the theatergoing public. But its possible indication of some diffidence on Garrick's part may have extended his feeling surrounding his first appearance at Ipswich that summer preceding, as the Negro slave Aboan in Southerne's *Oroonoko*, a role behind whose dark makeup Garrick may have been seeking to conceal his own identity.[72] Lloyd-Evans bolsters his argument in favor of Garrick's early reticence toward a career on the stage by speculating that the actor's choice of Richard III for his debut in London may have been influenced by the severity of the physical transformation required of those who undertook to play the hunchbacked king, and by Garrick's desire to hide himself in the role.[73]

In this connection, the naturalistic and contemporary components of Garrick's acting may have been balanced, at least initially, by his reflex—wedded to neoclassical esthetics—to objectify in some measure the roles he assumed. We shall look more closely at other sorts of balances which Garrick was to strike during his career in chapter 6; but particularly in an age caught up in the formulating and confirming of an idealized morality, Garrick may not have seen an advantage to having his personality associated in any way with the salient features of Aboan, a hothead and a revolutionary, or with those of Richard III.

In his first appearance on the stage, moreover, Garrick was fearful of his family's reaction to his new career. Even with both of his parents dead, he must have remained sensitive to the unsavory reputation of the acting profession and to the likelihood of disapproval from his brothers and sisters. His fears were justified. Brother Peter, who had become the head of the family when Captain Garrick died in 1737, seems to have been a stern man. Seven years older than David, Peter put up a firm resistance to his brother's intention to make a career on the stage, if we can judge his recalcitrance by the desperate and imploring tone of David's letters to him during the month which followed the first Richard III.[74] The anticipation of such resistance from other members of his family, in league with Peter, helps to explain Garrick's having waited until after his successful debut to inform his brother of his change in profession.

If, as Thomas Davies suggested, Garrick felt that his mother's death in 1740 had freed him to pursue an acting career,[75] a certain amount of guilt may have attended his earliest ventures onto the stage. The Garricks, as Huguenots and adoptive Englishmen, could, in V. S. Pritchett's phrase, "therefore be said to have been doubly bourgeois."[76] Garrick's desire to become an actor may have been qualified by two varieties of guilt: the first from a sense that he was somehow climbing to success on the stage over the wishes of his dead parents, and the second from the traditional antistage bias of most of the minor Protestant sects. Having once overcome these putative scruples, Garrick was never notably troubled by them. But the puritanical elements in his background may have resurfaced in the deprecating tone of many of his references to himself as an actor, reinforced also by the legacy of neoclassical esthetics and its antagonism toward the profession and practice of acting.

Two threads which run through Garrick's life—and which refer us continually to the childlike parts of the actor's personality—are his tendency to dramatize himself in every possible situation and his willingness to deal in public with his own private concerns. If at times these tendencies were self-serving, they seem also to have predated his choice of acting as a profession. Emblematic of these interrelated qualities is the first page of a diary which Garrick kept on his Grand Tour in the early 1760s, when the actor was in his mid-forties and far from the stage of the Drury Lane:

The following Journal is meant only to bring to my Mind hereafter the various things I shall see in my Journey into Italy—It may properly be call'd a Journal of my own Opinions & feelings, for I shall always write down my thought immediately as I am struck with different Objects, Customs, & Manners, without the least attention to what ~~might~~ [sic] has been said by ye many Writers of great or little reputation who have publish'd their Sentiments upon the same things.[77]

Garrick begins by proclaiming that the journal is for his own benefit, but gradually his sense of public, of posterity, and of occasion intrudes. His crossing out of the word *might* in his search for the most felicitous expression demonstrates the depth of his concern for the opinions of "the great world," together with his assumption that the journal could stand as a piece of literature on its own merits. The emendation also suggests that Garrick was measuring his insight as a traveler by the standards of other similar pieces which he had read, and that these hypothetical comparisons were present in his mind even before he began to compose his own journal. His protestation that he will not pay "the least attention" to other writers of such travel diaries savors of childish overstatement, as if he believed that a mere disclaimer would transform the appearance of indifference on his part into fact.

It may have been difficult for Garrick to do anything without some awareness of his place in society. His little introduction to his journal indicates his need to find form and meaning, always and clearly, in his own experience, and to render these in terms communicable to others. Even in a diary and far away from the stage, he seems to have created an audience of the mind, as a means of verifying and legitimizing his impressions of the world. In his persistent self-consciousness were wedded the instincts of the actor with the disposition of a precocious child. On March 18, 1742, Garrick followed his third appearance as King Lear—also his annual benefit performance in his first year on the stage—with another in the afterpiece, as Master Johnny, the title character in Colley Cibber's *The School Boy*.[78] The feat was a *tour de force*, but it stands also as an acting out of the duality at the heart of his nature—the archetypal man of family and the roguish and wayward schoolboy. This duality delighted many among his audience, but it confused and troubled others who expected more consistency, or at least a *different* consistency, from a man of Garrick's stature in the theater. In the next chapter we shall look at further instances of the confusion which his personality aroused.

NOTES

1. Joseph Knight, *David Garrick* (London: Kegan, Paul, Trench, Trübner & Co., Ltd., 1894), p. 296.

2. From Oliver Goldsmith "Retaliation" (1773); also in Carola Oman, *David Garrick* (Bungay, Suffolk: Hodder and Stoughton, 1958), pp. 328–29.

3. *The Rambler*, No. 200, February 15, 1752. Whether or not Johnson intended his piece as an attack on Garrick, Percy Fitzgerald wrote that Garrick had been offended by it when he read it. See Fitzgerald, *The Life of David Garrick*, rev. ed. (London: Simpkin, Marshall, Hamilton, Kent & Co., Ltd., 1899), p. 352.

4. Christopher Hibbert, *The Personal History of Samuel Johnson* (New York: Harper & Row, Publishers, 1971), p. 73.

5. Fitzgerald, *The Life of David Garrick*, p. 355.

6. "A Short Sketch of the Character and Writings of Mr. Garrick," *The Dramatic Works of David Garrick, Esq.* (London: Printed for R. Bald, T. Blaw, and J. Kert, 1774), I, viii.

7. Joshua Reynolds, *Portraits: Character Sketches of Goldsmith, Johnson, and Garrick*, ed. Frederick W. Hilles (New York: McGraw-Hill Book Company, Inc., 1952), p. 118.

8. Reynolds, *Portraits*, p. 119.

9. *The Letters of David Garrick*, ed. David M. Little and George M. Kahrl (Cambridge: Harvard University Press, 1963), II, 635.

10. *Lichtenberg's Visits to England*, trans. and ed. Margaret L. Mare and W. H. Quarrell (Oxford: The Clarendon Press, 1938), p. 7.

11. *The Letters of David Garrick*, I, 93; III, 915. See also Appendix F of George Winchester Stone, Jr., and George M. Kahrl, *David Garrick: A Critical Biography* (Carbondale: Southern Illinois University Press, 1979) pp. 672–73.

12. Thomas Davies, *Memoirs of the Life of David Garrick, Esq.* (London: Printed for the Author, 1780), I, 154.

13. Lucille S. Rubin, "Voices of the Past: David Garrick, John Philip Kemble, and Edmund Kean, 1741–1833" (Ph.D. dissertation, New York University, 1973), p. 161.

14. Fitzgerald, *The Life of David Garrick*, p. 42.

15. Thomas Davies, *Dramatic Miscellanies* (London: Printed for the Author, 1784), I, 225.

16. *The Letters of David Garrick*, III, 982.

17. Oman, *David Garrick*, p. 75.

18. Davies, *Memoirs*, I, 3.

19. *The Private Correspondence of David Garrick*, ed. James Boaden (London: Henry Colburn and Richard Bentley, 1831), I, 2.

20. Oman, *David Garrick*, p. 9.

21. *The Private Correspondence of David Garrick*, I, 2.

22. *The Letters of David Garrick*, I, 7.

23. Davies, *Memoirs*, I, 6–7.

24. *The Letters of David Garrick*, I, 2, 14–15.

25. *The Letters of David Garrick*, I, 14, 16, 19.

26. *The Letters of David Garrick*, I, 10.

27. Reynolds, *Portraits*, p. 97.

28. Davies, *Memoirs*, I, 4–5.

29. Included in this list of Garrick's roles as soldiers is every role in which explicit mention is made in the text of military occupation, or which clearly involves "soldierly" activity—such as planned and complex assaults, assassinations, or spying. In these latter cases, some degree of military skill or motive is implied in the refinement of the ac-

tivity. Garrick's soldierly roles, in the order in which he played them each for the first time, include:

1. Richard III
2. Chamont in *The Orphan* by Thomas Otway
3. Brazen in *The Recruiting Officer* by George Farquhar
4. Plume in *The Recruiting Officer*
5. Macbeth
6. Biron in *The Fatal Marriage* by Thomas Southerne
7. Zaphna in *Mahomet* by J. Miller and J. Hoadly
8. Othello
9. Faulconbridge in Shakespeare's *King John*
10. Iago
11. Orestes in *The Distrest Mother* by Ambrose Phillips
12. Hotspur in Shakespeare's *1 Henry IV*
13. Demetrius in *Irene* by Samuel Johnson
14. Eumenes/Dorilas in *Merope* by Aaron Hill
15. Edward in *Edward the Black Prince* by William Shirley
16. Horatius in *The Roman Father* by William Whitehead
17. Osmyn in *The Mourning Bride* by William Congreve
18. Alfred in *Alfred, A Masque* by David Mallet and James Thomson
19. Demetrius in *The Brothers* by Edward Young
20. Dumnorix in *Boadicea* by Richard Glover
21. Don John in *The Chances* by John Fletcher
22. Achmet in *Barbarossa* by John Brown
23. Athelstan in *Athelstan* by John Brown
24. Leon in *Rule a Wife and Have a Wife* by John Fletcher
25. Don Felix in *The Wonder* by Susannah Centlivre
26. Lysander in *Agis* by John Home
27. King Henry in Shakespeare's *2 Henry IV*
28. Periander in *Eurydice* by David Mallet
29. Oroonoko in *Oroonoko* by Thomas Southerne
30. Aemilius in *The Siege of Aquileia* by John Home.

30. Oman, *David Garrick*, pp. 81–82.
31. In *A Biographical Dictionary of Actors . . . in London, 1660–1800,* vol. 6 (Carbondale: Southern Illinois University Press, 1978), Philip H. Highfill, Jr., et al. refer to Captain Garrick as an "indulgent and un-

derstanding father" (p. 2). They may be right, but the fragmentary evidence seems to suggest that David may not have seen his father in quite so kindly a light.

32. *The Letters of David Garrick*, I, 9.

33. *The Letters of David Garrick*, I, 16.

34. Percival Stockdale, *Memoirs*, II, 137ff.; cited in *The Letters of David Garrick*, I, 23n.

35. Stone and Kahrl, *David Garrick*, p. 13. In their *Biographical Dictionary of Actors* Highfill et al. state that Garrick left Lichfield *nine days* before Captain Garrick's funeral. There are similar disagreements among scholars about David's age at the time of his childhood trip to Portugal.

36. Stone and Kahrl, *David Garrick*, p. 5.

37. *The Letters of David Garrick*, I, xxvi.

38. J. H. Plumb, "The New World of Children in Eighteenth-Century England," *Past and Present*, 67 (1975), 64–95.

39. Lawrence Stone, *The Family, Sex and Marriage in England 1500–1800* (New York: Harper & Row, 1977), p. 405.

40. Stone and Kahrl, *David Garrick*, pp. 473, 590.

41. See Stone and Kahrl, *David Garrick*, Appendix D, pp. 661–62.

42. Margaret Barton, *Garrick* (London: Faber and Faber, 1949), p. 117.

43. *The Letters of David Garrick*, I, 28.

44. *The Letters of David Garrick*, I, 31.

45. *The Letters of David Garrick*, I, 39.

46. *The Letters of David Garrick*, I, 40.

47. Oman, *David Garrick*, p. 54.

48. *The Letters of David Garrick*, I, 387.

49. *The Letters of David Garrick*, I, 28.

50. *The Letters of David Garrick*, I, 37.

51. See Appendix C of Leigh Woods, "David Garrick and the Actor's Means: A Revolution in Acting-Style, in Relation to the Life of the Times" (Ph.D. dissertation, University of California, Berkeley, 1979), p. 384.

52. Fitzgerald, *The Life of David Garrick*, p. 129.

53. Fitzgerald, *The Life of David Garrick*, pp. 203–4.

54. Reynolds, *Portraits*, p. 109.

55. Tate Wilkinson, *Memoirs of His Own Life* (York, 1790), II, 81; cited in Christian Deelman, *The Great Shakespeare Jubilee* (New York: The Viking Press, 1964), p. 87.

56. John Hill, *The Actor: A Treatise on the Art of Acting* (London, 1750), p. 309.

57. Davies, *Memoirs*, II, 382.

58. Fitzgerald, *The Life of David Garrick*, p. 161.

59. Oman, *David Garrick*, pp. 173–75.

60. Oman, *David Garrick*, pp. 223–24.

61. See Appendix C in Stone and Kahrl, *David Garrick*, pp. 659–60, and Appendix C of Woods, "David Garrick and the Actor's Means," p. 384. See also chapter 3, note 21, in this book for reasons why some of my performance figures for Garrick may differ slightly from those of Stone and Kahrl.

62. Fitzgerald, *The Life of David Garrick*, pp. 282–83.

63. *The Letters of David Garrick*, II, 435–36.

64. See Harry C. Payne, "Elite versus Popular Mentality in the Eighteenth Century," *Studies in Eighteenth-Century Culture*, vol. 8, ed. Roseann Runte (Madison: University of Wisconsin Press, 1979), pp. 3–32; and George Rudé, *Paris and London in the Eighteenth Century: Studies in Popular Protest* (New York: The Viking Press, 1952).

65. Stone and Kahrl, *David Garrick*, pp. 136–37.

66. Spoken as the character of Busy Body in "Address to the Town," *The Poetical Works of David Garrick, Esq.* (London: Printed for George Kearsley, 1785), I, 192.

67. Cited in Fitzgerald, *The Life of David Garrick*, p. 303.

68. *The Poetical Works of David Garrick*, I, 52.

69. Mary E. Knapp, "Garrick's Last Command Performance," *The Age of Johnson: Essays Presented to Chauncey Brewster Tinker* (New Haven: Yale University Press, 1949), p. 70.

70. Knapp, "Garrick's Last Command Performance," p. 69.

71. Gareth Lloyd-Evans, "Garrick and the 18th-Century Theatre," *The Johnson Society Transactions*, December 1965, 19.

72. Davies, *Memoirs*, I, 17; Arthur Murphy, *The Life of David Garrick, Esq.* (London: J. F. Foot, 1801), I, 19. Percy Fitzgerald, in *The Life of David Garrick*, p. 36, also imputes Garrick's choice of Aboan to his desire for anonymity, and he adds to his opinion the testimony of a descendant of Henry Giffard, who had hired Garrick to act at Ipswich and served as his first acting teacher.

73. Lloyd-Evans, "Garrick and the 18th-Century Theatre," 19.

74. *The Letters of David Garrick*, I, 27–33.

75. Davies, *Memoirs*, I, 15.

76. V. S. Pritchett, "The Unfrogged Frenchman," *New Statesman*, LXVIII (1964), 167.

77. *The Journal of David Garrick Describing His Visit to France and Italy in 1763*, ed. George Winchester Stone, Jr. (New York: The Modern Language Association of America, 1939), p. 3.

78. *The London Stage, 1729–1747*, Part 3, ed. Arthur H. Scouten (Carbondale: Southern Illinois University Press, 1961), p. 976.

Garrick as Hamlet, by Benjamin Wilson. From the Art Collection of the Folger Shakespeare Library.

5

Managing the Theater, Managing the World

Garrick's rival and fellow-actor, Thomas Sheridan, in a conversation once with Boswell spoke of the presence of calculation and of the lack of genuine emotional involvement in Garrick's acting. Sheridan was only repeating the most common and telling criticism of Garrick's work on the stage with his claim to Boswell that "Garrick had no real feeling; that his talents for mimicry enabled him to put on the appearance of feeling, and that the nicety of his art might please the fancy and make us cry, 'That's fine.' But as it was art, it could never touch the heart."[1] And, as we have seen already, the same calculation ascribed to Garrick in the practice of his acting was often attributed to him in the conduct of his personal life, too. The Countess Spencer once complained to the actor about his lack of spontaneity in his recent correspondence with her: "I have no great partiality for studied letters, nor do I much admire those you have sent."[2] Samuel Johnson told Fanny Burney that "Garrick never enters a room, but he regards himself as the object of general attention, from which the entertainment of the company is expected . . . he thinks it so incumbent upon him to be sportive, that his gaiety becomes mechanical . . . and he can exert his spirits at all times alike."[3] Such comments from sources both friendly and antagonistic to the actor reinforce the sense that Garrick was a manager by nature, as well as by title. This chapter examines the varieties which his managing assumed.

SELF-PROMOTION

Whether generated by his sense of obligation or by the self-serving need for attention and praise, Garrick's attempts at managing his world were not confined to the stage and to the drawing rooms of his friends. In dealing with criticism, in particular, Garrick manifested a tendency to anticipate it, to identify the quarter from which it came, and to state it himself in either diluted or comically disproportionate terms. We have seen already an example of this tendency, in Garrick's writing of "The Sick Monkey," a case in which he must have known that his return to London after an absence of a year and one-half would be greeted with nearly unanimous enthusiasm. But for Garrick, it seems, nothing short of unanimous enthusiasm for himself and his efforts was sufficient.

Thomas Davies felt that "Garrick's ruling passion was the love of fame."[4] Arthur Murphy, Garrick's second biographer and acquainted with Garrick through his own success as a playwright, pointedly echoes Davies's assessment with his assertion that "the love of fame was Garrick's ruling passion, even to anxiety."[5] Garrick's pursuit of fame is very evident in his social dealings. He was on familiar terms with many of the most prominent people in Britain, and he cultivated such contacts with a fervor which suggests that they stood, for him, as the proofs of his eminence. He gained the favor and protection (not to mention the dowry) of the Count and Countess Burlington when he married their ward, the Austrian dancer Veigel.[6] He was friendly with Lord Hertford, who after 1766 was the Lord Chamberlain and, hence, official censor for all plays submitted for performance at the London patent theaters.[7] Having met the future Count and Countess Spencer on his travels to Italy, he would remain close to them and their family for the rest of his life. He seems to have taken care in his long correspondence with the Countess Spencer to represent himself as a man of letters and society and to ignore almost entirely his connection to the theater.

Nor was his instinct for self-publicizing confined to its exercise among the titled and the socially prominent. When Garrick's widow comforted Edmund Kean over several unfavorable reviews he had received many years after her husband's death, she tried to bolster Kean up with the news that David had not needed to concern himself with bad reviews very often because he had been able to write his own.[8] Well known in Garrick's time on the stage, the practice of "puffing" consisted in a playwright's or a manager's writing favorable notices and circulating these as anonymous accounts. Garrick seems to have turned this practice into a high art, and he was certainly aided in this by his acquaintance among journalists and by his being in a position, as manager of one of two patent theaters in London, to offer favors to these men whenever he needed one in return.

His own *An Essay on Acting*, printed shortly after his first appearance as Macbeth, demonstrates Garrick's turn for recommending the virtues of his acting. Like "The Sick Monkey" published without attribution, Garrick adopted a satirical stance toward himself and his acting rivals, as the surface of the piece "praises" his competitors and mocks himself. He writes of "Macbeth Burlesqu'd, or Begarrick'd," and he refers to himself in the role as "the Anticlimax of, or rather the Antipode of Shakespeare."[9] He concludes his introduction with the promise to "present my Readers with the following short treatise upon ACTING, which will show 'em what ACTING ought to be, and what the present Favourite in Question [referring to himself] is not."[10] Even as he criticized himself, though, Garrick was gathering his readers' credence in the real thrust of his attack—at the Macbeth of his major rival, James Quin.

Garrick's ironic and anonymous approach in the *Essay* enabled him to avoid offering any direct criticism of Quin's Macbeth, at the same time that it was making that performance the butt of its satire. Garrick's Macbeth was characterized by its inner tension and economy during the early scenes, and these features are entirely consistent with his description of the character in the *Essay* as a "moving statue" in the moments following the murder of Duncan. But Garrick "cautions" aspiring actors against imitating his own acting of the role, and he "recommends" Quin's manner instead. What emerges from such tongue-in-cheek advice is a kind of cutting enthusiasm for Quin's performance, devastating because it is so obviously unfounded:

He should not rivet his Eye to an imaginary Object, as if it really was there [in Garrick's manner], but should shew an unsettled Motion in his Eye, like one not quite awak'd from some disordering Dream; his hands and fingers should not be immoveable, but restless, and endeavouring to disperse the Cloud that over shadows his optick Ray, and bedims his Intellects; here would be Confusion, Disorder, and Agony! "Come, let me clutch thee!" is not to be done by one Motion only, but by several successive Catches at it, first with one Hand, and then with the other, preserving the same Motion, at the same Time, with his Feet, like a Man, who out of his Depth, and half drowned in his Struggles, catches at Air for Substance. This would make the Spectator's Blood run cold, and he would almost feel the Agonies of the Murderer himself.[11]

We see that in undertaking the role of Macbeth, Garrick had calculated his own efforts as an actor to make them seem original, as we would expect him to do, but that he also tried to influence the critical response to his own playing of the role by satirizing the major competing characterization, labeling it with the same accusation of busyness which he had often heard applied to his own acting by 1744. Perhaps Quin had borrowed a page from Garrick with his crazed and shuffling Macbeth; perhaps Garrick had refined Quin's style in his own more stationary playing. In any event, Garrick the actor had Garrick the writer to shape his own reputation in the stages of its unfolding, and this was an advantage Quin lacked.

IMAGE-SHAPING

Garrick also wrote plays and acted in them, on occasion, and the sequence of his roles in his own plays supplies us with perhaps the most informative pictures of his attempts to influence popular opinions toward himself. In his first season on the stage, his fifth role came as Sharp in his own afterpiece, *The Lying Valet*. How might Garrick have seen the role of a crafty, conniving servant as one which could sustain and enhance his popularity?

It may be that in writing the role of a valet and casting himself in it, Garrick was seeking to humble himself, after a fashion, in the wake of his first spectacular successes. But by making Sharp calculating and leaving him unrepentant at the end of the play, after having been revealed as a selfish plotter, Garrick seems to have been balancing a gesture of abjection in his impersonation of a servant with one of independence, in his stubborness and consistency as Sharp. If Garrick felt he had risen to prominence in the London theater-world by his own wits and talents, Sharp may embody some attempt on his part to ease his audience's possible resentment toward him, at the same time that it dramatizes his own uncertainty about that audience and the steadfastness of its approval.

At the end of *The Lying Valet*, circumstances are brought about which reveal Sharp in all his machinations, but he is then forgiven by the other characters, whom he has attempted to deceive, and let off with only a warning. The play is a comedy, and its *dramatis personae* find a way to accommodate the wily but essentially harmless scoundrel. And Garrick, perhaps, was seeking a way to criticize his own "sharpness," to transform it into the stuff of laughter, and so to render it inoffensive and even appealing to his audience. *The Lying Valet* and Garrick's Sharp stand as social organisms as well as theatrical ones, in the sense that with them Garrick was searching for ways to influence popular reaction to his new fame as much as to his acting.

Early in 1747, he wrote for himself the role of Fribble in *Miss in Her Teens*, another afterpiece. The season in which the play appeared was to be the final one before Garrick assumed the managership and patent at Drury Lane, and during much of this 1746–47 season he was caught up in negotiations concerning the terms on which he would enter into partnership with James Lacy for the control of one of London's two royal theaters.[12]

As Fribble, Garrick painted himself as a supremely ineffectual, foppish suitor, more effeminate, indeed, than the lady whom he courts. Garrick's purpose in writing and playing Fribble seems to have been a double one. Again, as with Sharp, he seems to have been seeking to trivialize his image, with an eye to countering any public alarm at his growing influence which the imminent succession to the royal patent may have aroused. He may also have been trying to moderate the public's sense of him as a charmer and manipulator in his personal affairs, an image which had reared itself first in minds like Horace Walpole's and which had likely been given more substance during the time of his three-year liaison with the beautiful though promiscuous actress, Peg Woffington.

Nor was Fribble to be the only rejected suitor Garrick played during the 1746–47 season. He also undertook the role of Ranger in his friend Benjamin Hoadly's play, *The Suspicious Husband*. Ranger is a would-be rake who is revealed by the events of the play to be hopelessly ineffectual in his efforts at seduction and is exposed at the end as a man who has led a life of involuntary and humiliating celibacy. Garrick undertook both Ranger and Fribble at a time when he was preparing to accept a position of responsibility and influence in the London theater, and conventional expectation would have had him trying to paint himself in colors as sober, responsible, and dignified as possible, even as his mentor Gilbert Walmesley had done in his recommendation of Garrick some ten years earlier. Instead, Garrick resorted characteristically to self-deprecation, and although neither Fribble nor Ranger stands as a model of middle-class dignity, each may have gone toward erasing any lingering image of the schemer and the rake which surrounded Garrick's private life. Both characters are exposed at the end of the plays which contain them, Fribble in his cowardice and Ranger in his ridiculous need to represent himself as a profligate. It was as if Garrick in these roles sought to expose himself, too, in some new light; and by creating Ranger and Fribble he seems to have been looking to deflect his audience's concern from his role as a public figure to his role as a private man, and to refer playgoers from the issue of ambition to that of personal deportment.

In 1756, Garrick wrote a new part for himself in his first play, *Lethe*. He had written the first version of the play in 1740, before he had begun to act at all, and he revised the play repeatedly during his career, often updating it with fresh topical material. The role of Lord Chalkstone (colloquial for "kidneystone"), a wealthy, affected, and physically debilitated nobleman, seems to represent Garrick's attempt to soften some of the resentment which attended his growing wealth and social standing. This motive, in fact, consistently seems to underlie Garrick's creation of roles for himself, and it helps to explain the persistent self-deflation which we see at work, to a greater or lesser extent, in each of the roles.

The three roles he had undertaken in his 1749 production of *Lethe*—a Poet, a Drunken Man, and a Frenchman—were all pictures of poor and disadvantaged men. But in 1754, Garrick had bought his country estate at Hampton, and in the aftermath of his succession to the patent at Drury Lane, he had found himself courted even more assiduously than before by the wealthy and titled. His sponsorship of Noverre's "The Chinese Festival" in 1755 had precipitated severe Francophobic rioting in his theater, and it had also implicated Garrick as a member of the generally French-loving cultured elite. By 1756, with Britain and France at war, it may have been to Garrick's advantage to erase in particular the public's memory of himself as the Frenchman in *Lethe* which, to judge it from its more frequent performances, had been the best received of the three roles Garrick had played in 1749.[13]

As the slave to fad and fashion, the character of Lord Chalkstone referred the audience toward Garrick's increasing social access, but it also drew compelling contrasts between Chalkstone's selfishness and laziness and Garrick's well-known industry and public-spiritedness. In creating the character, especially in a play which had first brought his name before the theatergoing public, it is as if Garrick was seeking to reassure his audience that he was aware of the dangers of wealth when mingled with self-indulgence and would never himself fall victim to them.

But if this is indeed something of what Garrick intended, his purpose once again was realized through a kind of indirection. As Chalkstone, Garrick assumed the manners and behavior of an affected, amoral aristocrat, and so admitted his own familiarity with the species; however, his portrayal of the character drew the audience's laughter and ridicule on Lord Chalkstone, and in this way Garrick may have been able to capitalize on the same suspicions of elitism and snobbery which he felt previously had been directed at himself.

In 1762, a similarly deflective impulse seems to have been at work in Garrick, although it seems to have found a rather different vehicle for its expression. In a short interlude (only about

four pages long) titled *The Farmer's Return from London*, the role
of the rustic Farmer appears to have offered Garrick the opportunity of reminding his audience of his own roots in provincial Lichfield. The Farmer, as he is drawn in the play, is entirely divorced from the affectations and corruptions he has
witnessed while in London. Having just returned from his trip
to the great city, he delights in amazing his wife and children
with tales of a metropolis they have never seen. Among the evils
and curiosities he describes to his family in rolling verse are the
streetwalkers, the silly, striving wits, the court dandies, the theater
audiences who attend plays in order to be seen rather than to
see, and the perpetually grumbling theater critics, whom nothing can please.[14]

As with Lord Chalkstone, Garrick may have been looking for
a way of disassociating himself from the license and abandon
which characterized segments of London society. By means of
the Farmer's naive yet pointed observations about the preten-
tiousness and artificiality of city customs, Garrick may have been
seeking to reassure his audience—the largest part of which was
middle-class people—that he still shared their spirit of austerity
and sacrifice, and that he was critical of the same abuses and
affectations which offended them. The more that Garrick moved
within the upper levels of English society, the more care he may
have taken to remind his public that he had come from a small
town and from a humble but honorable family. If Lord Chalkstone accomplished this aim by indirection, then the Farmer may
have represented a more direct and mature statement of Garrick's purpose, and of the values with which he was seeking to
associate himself.

Garrick's role in a fifth play of his own composition came as
Heartly in *The Guardian*, a play written three years before *The
Farmer's Return from London*. Garrick's "Heartly" is the title role
in the afterpiece, a middle-aged man who had been entrusted
with the care of the orphaned Harriet when she was only a small
child some years before. Sensing in her lately the wish to marry,
and having come to see her himself as a beautiful young woman,
Heartly conscientiously searches for an agreeable mate for her.
The match he helps to arrange is rejected by Harriet; and finally, when the sensible but tongue-tied ward is able to over-

come her embarrassment and reveal her own choice for a husband, she tells him of her love for him, Heartly, her guardian. For his own part, of course, he has loved her for some while but has refused to reveal his own inclinations out of a surfeit of the same sort of "feeling" which prevented Harriet from speaking out for so long. Fortunately, the same feeling that kept them apart finally unites them, as an ideally matched sentimental couple.

On one level, Garrick seems to have written the part as a way of effecting for himself, at the age of forty-two, a graceful transition from young romantic roles to older domesticated ones. After playing Heartly, Garrick's repertoire was to grow more heavily seasoned with middle-aged and old men: eight, from a total of fourteen new roles which he took after Heartly, were either fathers or father-surrogates, and one more was a comically superannuated suitor.[15]

Garrick also created a character in Heartly which combined feeling with responsibility and which functioned in some senses both as a lover and as a father-figure. By endowing Heartly with this sort of dual capacity (which Garrick later recapitulated in a full-length play with his acting of Sir John Dorilant in Whitehead's *The School for Lovers*), Garrick affirmed his belief that a man could be both spontaneous and sensitive to others, emotionally expressive and socially responsible at the same time.

Heartly was a dramatic image for a combination of qualities Garrick may have wished for or perceived in himself. The character is both a parody and a rationalization of a kind of managing of one's emotions toward altruistic ends. The play is deeply and self-consciously sentimental, both in our sense of the word and in the eighteenth century's. But it strikes a more sober chord than do any of Garrick's other plays in which he also took roles, in its representation of a species of behavior—in "heartliness"—which Garrick seems to have admired.[16]

Garrick's roles in plays of his own composing provide a valuable perspective on his attempts to influence his own public image. Because these roles were entirely the products of his own imagination and execution, we may look upon them as responses to the changing circumstances of his personal popularity. In plays written by other authors, even when the playwrights were, like John and Benjamin Hoadly, his close friends, the degree of Garrick's control was never so total as it was in productions of plays he wrote and acted. In his own plays, too, Garrick was free to structure the entire play around the role he coveted for himself, even though Fribble and Lord Chalkstone among the roles just examined are not the central characters in the plays which contain them.

Each of the roles is self-deprecatory in a different way, and Garrick as a public figure seems to have been using this puncturing of certain popularly conceived notions of himself as a means of softening the impact of his growing fame and influence. Sharp is without scruples and he is defeated in his plotting, although he refuses to reform his devious nature. Fribble is without courage and he fails miserably as a suitor, although he succeeds in escaping injury at the hands of one of his jealous rivals. Lord Chalkstone is self-absorbed and isolated, and he is exposed by the satirical tone of *Lethe* and by his own actions within it as a callous, ignorant, and irresponsible person. The Farmer is a bumpkin, although a perceptive social critic. And Heartly is a character who practices the virtues of self-abnegation, but who by the end of the play wins what he most wants. Each of these characters, except Lord Chalkstone, is described by a fundamental polarity, and each in this sense offers another instance of Garrick's fondness for "cross-grained" drawing of dramatic character. And if we again except Lord Chalkstone, each character has one side which works to make him seem ridiculous and another side which works to attach him to the audience's sympathies.

The plays which contain these characters are comedies, as were all the plays Garrick wrote. Comedy was the ideal medium for managing his public image to his own advantage. When Garrick wrote a character which mocked some aspect of his own person—at least as it was perceived in the public mind—he was seeking to anticipate his critics' barbs and to disarm their criticism entirely if he could by celebrating his ability to laugh at himself. He could ridicule himself as a playwright and then, as an actor, he could participate in the laughter he had succeeded in arousing. This inclination toward self-ridicule is the instinct of the clown, and it was perhaps logical that observers like Walpole, Theophilus Cibber, and Samuel Johnson compared Garrick to the clowns they had seen, although their descriptions this way tended to incorporate unflattering connotations. What these critics also saw, and what seems to have irritated them, was the extent to which Garrick's ridiculing of himself was in fact a rather clever and deft form of self-promotion.

Garrick's managing of his public image offers a clear picture of his need for universal acceptance. His desire for such acceptance was spectacularly unrealistic for a man in his position, but his inevitable failures to achieve it seem only to have spurred him to work even harder for it, and to "manage" more. During his first season as an actor, he comanaged the Goodman's Fields theater with Henry Giffard, and during the last thirty years of his career he was the acting manager at Drury Lane, a job which entailed the selection of a large acting company, the scheduling of the season, and the casting and directing of all plays performed there. Consequently, in all but five of his complete seasons on the stage (1742–43 through 1746–47, inclusive), Garrick was in a position to cast himself in whatever roles he wished, so long as he did not take away a role claimed already by one of the other leading actors in his company, and to appear in whatever plays he chose to produce, provided that in his judgment such plays contained the possibility of commercial success. In short, the only limitations on his freedom to dispose himself as he wished within the Drury Lane repertory came from the respect he felt toward the other fine actors in his company, and from the shifting tastes of his public. Even in this, though, he was capable of guiding taste to a considerable extent through his decisions as manager on what to play and when and whom to play it, as well as through his decisions as a leading actor about how to play it.

He had strong ideas about the proper role and conduct of the theater, and he was never one for letting others make decisions for him, even though he might shrink at times from making them at the moment or on demand. He was not only the product of his time and its tastes, but to some extent their arbiter, too, in matters theatrical and in the resonances of the theater in contemporary life. What he had the chance to influence or control, whether it was his interpretations of roles, his repertoire, his popularity, his reviews, or his image, he did—or at least he tried to. Our greatest puzzlement may come in trying to understand how he was able to do so much. The amount of energy he must have possessed in order to address the many challenges to his resourcefulness and judgment can only elaborate our sense of what it was that he brought onto the stage with him which made him so compelling to watch.

THE IMAGE IN ACTION

An Essay on Acting, as we have seen, attests to Garrick's constant and conscious resort to an external, behavioristic image of dramatic character. A seasoning of sympathy and sentiment worked to soften the potentially mechanistic quality which such an approach to character embodied. But Garrick's inclination toward managing all areas of his life applied itself to his acting in an approach to his roles based on an active search for their physical life, and the persistence of this search was qualified not at all by sentimentalism. In Garrick's acting, this aggressive searching out of physical actions which could describe a character took precedence over structural analyses of his roles, or exhaustive comparisons between "their" experience and his of the sort which accompanied the advent of Romanticism. The workings of sympathetic imagination were, in this sense, largely physical, for both the actor and the audience; and this meaning of *sympathy* is one which has largely been effaced by the lapse of time between Garrick's age and our own.

The particular physical actions and types of movement and speech Garrick used in his characters must have derived directly from his experience of the world. Apart from his acknowledged use as King Lear of his recollections of a friend's madness induced after having accidentally dropped an infant daughter to her death through an open window,[17] Garrick seems to have been most frequently given to creating his characters in patchwork fashion, from random and fleeting impressions of people he had seen. Several stories testify, for instance, to his fondness for frequenting courtrooms, in search of models for moments in his characterizations.[18] Still another has him purposely creating a row among a group of schoolboys in order to observe their reactions at first hand, as he stood safely beyond the fray.[19]

This kind of management, if Garrick indeed practiced it, seems calculating in the extreme. On the other hand, it was Garrick's conscious technique as an actor and his ability to calculate his effects in their precise impact on an audience which enabled him to create and sustain many of his most powerful moments. His Hamlet-start, for example, in its famous description by the German George Lichtenberg, would have been impossible without elaborate planning and rehearsal:

Suddenly, as Hamlet moves towards the back of the stage slightly to the left and turns his back on the audience, Horatio starts, and saying: "Look, my lord, it comes," points to the right, where the ghost has already appeared and stands motionless, before any one is aware of him. At these words Garrick turns sharply and at the same moment staggers back two or three paces with his knees giving way under him; his hat falls to the ground and both his arms, especially the left, are stretched out nearly to their full length, with the hands as high as his head, the right arm more bent and the hand lower, and the fingers apart; his mouth is open; thus he stands rooted to the spot, with legs apart, but no loss of dignity, supported by his friends, who are better acquainted with the apparition and fear lest he should collapse.[20]

A considerable degree of planning and calculation must have gone especially into the backward, blind stagger and the supported near-fall.

Garrick's concern with technical detail such as that in evidence in his Hamlet-start had the virtue of endowing his acting with a certain consistency, especially necessary at its moments of peak emotional intensity, either to supply the appearance of feeling when true inspiration may have been absent or to regulate the actor's sympathetic feeling when it threatened to spiral out of control. In a sense, Garrick was doubly armed to render key moments in a characterization, by his elaborate physical preparation and by his conscious cultivation of the circumstances for extreme sympathetic identification. In fact, Garrick's apparently heightened sensitivity to kinesthetic detail may have worked to free him from the burden of conscious thought at certain moments on the stage, and so facilitated his movement toward the state of extreme sympathy which he termed "transport" in his letter criticizing the French actress Clairon.[21] Once he had realized such a moment in a way that satisfied him, he seems to have worked to preserve it in its essential contours. The unfinished painting of Garrick's Hamlet-start by Benjamin Wilson corroborates the accuracy of Lichtenberg's account of the moment and argues that the start stayed much the same over a period of years. (See illustration, p. 106.)

Even as he worked to create and refine such moments, Garrick appears to have done everything in his power to portray his acting as the result primarily of feeling and of spontaneity. His apparent reluctance to endorse Diderot's image of the ideal actor as an artist essentially detached from the character he portrays may have owed to Garrick's conviction that technique and a command of physical action on the stage were not sufficient to produce great acting.[22] Perhaps he feared that his approval of Diderot's *Paradoxe sur le comédien* might lend credence to the image of his acting advanced by Johnson, Theophilus Cibber, Thomas Sheridan, and Horace Walpole, to whom all of his effects seemed studied. A conviction of absolute control on the actor's part tends, after all, to call attention to elements of shaping and volition at the expense of the audience's sympathetic involvement in the play. Heightened degrees of this involvement, of course, were the responses Garrick was most interested in arousing always in tragedy, and even at times in comedy.

Diderot's image of actors' personalities was not a flattering one, either. He felt that actors tended to be men with little or no character of their own, precisely because their work required them to assimilate all characters.[23] He saw actors as superficial and insubstantial people in their offstage lives, although he admitted that they often made witty and engaging companions. These criticisms, it should be noted, bear a striking resemblance to those which were leveled against Garrick by Johnson and Walpole. Curiously enough, Diderot met Garrick on the actor's visit to Paris during 1764–65, used him as the epitome of the approach to acting which he recommended in his *Paradoxe*, and respected him enough as an artist and critic to solicit, through an intermediary, his opinion of the *Paradoxe*.[24] It is not difficult to understand why Garrick may have been reluctant to embrace the image of the aloof, mechanical, and shallow actor Diderot had fashioned, no matter how sound he might have thought the speculations on the actor's work which the *Paradoxe* contained—in the event that he read it at all.

For an actor to describe his methods or call his audience's attention to them would amount to his giving up of trade secrets and sacrificing his capacity to inspire a suspension of disbelief among his audience. An audience made aware of components of technical control will be scrutinizing the actor for precisely those elements which any actor working within a naturalistic framework is seeking to disguise. To an uninitiated spectator, the word *technique* suggests that the actor who employs it is working out of a structure of artifice, above all. Particularly in the atmosphere of self-conscious sincerity which attached to the theater in Garrick's time, and which he helped both to foster and to perpetuate, it would have been to his advantage to conceal his technical awareness and facility behind an appearance of nearly total spontaneity and emotional vulnerability, in character.

The infusions of empirical psychology and naturalism which accompanied Garrick's debut demanded a disguised technique, and this new demand worked in turn to distinguish Garrick's acting from the styles of the leading declamatory actors who had preceded him on the English stage. Actors such as Betterton and Quin had performed with an eye to celebrating and to some extent parading their skills as speakers. They had shared with their audiences a view of tragic acting, in particular, as a form of expression distinct in some ways from the quality of expression in everyday life. Because these actors were not considered to have been exercising any independent creative function in their neoclassical charge of merely rendering the text that was given to them, and because their profession was considered to be inherently demeaning, they seem to have been regarded in much the same light as were athletes or musicians—as the possessors of certain specialized skills whose demonstration an audience expected in return for the price of admission to the theater.

In the wake of Garrick's debut, many actors came to feel a growing pressure to soften the older declamatory techniques, to moderate the older tragic "strutting" and posturing, and to subordinate such refined vocal and physical skills as they possessed to a surface of behavior which approximated more closely that of ordinary men and women. As almost certainly the most physically acute and adept actor of his day, Garrick may have felt an added necessity of minimizing the role kinesthetic skill played in his acting. His strategy in this may not have involved any willful distorting of his art, but rather a selective and figurative way of describing it which would make it more accessible to his public. Through all of this, Garrick continued to devise new effects and to rehearse them meticulously. As Hamlet, for instance, his hair would stand on end at his first sight of his father's ghost, thanks to the assistance of a special wig that he commissioned, the hairs of which were activated by a small mechanical device which he hid in his costume.[25]

Garrick's technical control and his interest in elaborate effects offer only a partial image of his style. His impromptu entertaining as a child, his skills as a pantomimist, and his witty private conversation all demonstrate his gift for improvisation and variety. Nor was Garrick content merely to reproduce earlier performances he had given in a role in photographic fashion; he looked always for original and improved stage business and for the new emotional overtones which would attend it. His correspondence after 1765 includes several references to his anticipation and nervousness in the days before he was to play an especially demanding role.[26] And at times this nervousness seems to have arisen as the result of his attempt to perform new business or to break in a new costume in public.[27]

In earlier years, it seems that the weight of business affairs, together with the constant pressure of learning and rehearsing new roles, often had the effect of relegating Garrick's acting to its exercise only in rehearsals and performance. After 1765, when he no longer took on new roles, neither did he play ever again more than thirteen roles in a single season, down from his peak number of twenty-nine.[28] The combination of fewer roles and fewer total performances seems to have brought him to regard each chance to act as a separate and increasingly treasured opportunity. In this connection, at least, Garrick's managing worked to benefit himself and, we may guess, those playgoers who were lucky enough to see him when he did perform.

In another sense, "managing" was embodied in his thorough and systematic ways of creating dramatic characters on the stage. In his *An Essay on Acting* he had proclaimed that his motives as a critic were "merely Scientifical";[29] and even if this statement was not entirely straightforward, it signals Garrick's respect for scientific rigor and his belief that it could be applied to the practice of acting. Learning the lines for any of his characters was only the shortest and simplest step in his search for truth and the lifelike as they might reveal themselves in physical action. Science and application discovered vivid and distinct actions for each character, and the imaginative energy born of sympathetic identification knitted them together into the illusion of a real person. A certain kind and degree of managing were necessary in this connection in order to create the conditions for sympathy in his audience, if not always, necessarily, in himself.

Finally, in his thoroughness as a "manager" in the broad sense and his preoccupation with its exercises, Garrick embodied the self-reliance and pragmatism which were leading features of the Enlightenment. The empirical revolution in science was manifesting itself in other areas of endeavor, in its emphasis on experiment and observation. If it generated a measure of hesitance in regard to affirming and passing along older religious ideas, it raised a new sort of confidence, too, in its implicit encouragement of venturing, and in its affirmation that the consequences even of mistaken action could be reversed or remedied with repeated trials. Among its results were a broader faith in the capacity of men to influence their own destinies, and in the essential progress of human history. We shall look in chapter 6 at the degree to which these ideals were both realized on and subverted by Garrick's stage.

NOTES

1. James Boswell, *Boswell's London Journal, 1762–1763*, ed. Frederick A. Pottle (New York: McGraw-Hill Book Company, Inc., 1950), p. 57.

2. Cited in Edward Wagenknecht, *Merely Players* (Norman: University of Oklahoma Press, 1966), p. 21.

3. The Early Diary of Frances Burney, 1768–1778," ed. A. R. Ellis, rev. ed. (London, 1907), II, 158; cited in Christian Deelman, *The Great Shakespeare Jubilee* (New York: The Viking Press, 1964), p. 86.

4. Thomas Davies, *Memoirs of the Life of David Garrick, Esq.* (London: Printed for the Author, 1780), I, 293.

5. Arthur Murphy, *The Life of David Garrick, Esq.* (London: J. F. Foot, 1801), II, 13.

6. Murphy, *The Life of David Garrick*, I, 172. It must be added that Garrick was enamoured of the beautiful "Violette" and that he was the most devoted of husbands to her. (See chapter 4, text identified by note 52.) Garrick did not make merely a politically advantageous and financially profitable match, although his choice of a bride did not harm him in these respects, either.

7. *The Letters of David Garrick*, ed. David M. Little and George M. Kahrl (Cambridge: Harvard University Press, 1963), III, 1309, 1312.

8. Charles Harold Gray, *Theatrical Criticism in London to 1795* (New York: Columbia University Press, 1931), p. 201.

9. David Garrick, *An Essay on Acting* (London, 1744), p. 2.

10. Garrick, *Essay*, p. 3.

11. Garrick, *Essay*, pp. 17–18.

12. Carola Oman, *David Garrick* (Bungay, Suffolk: Hodder and Stoughton, 1958), pp. 98–99.

13. Garrick performed the Frenchman fourteen times in 1748–49 and two more times each in the 1749–50 and 1751–52 seasons, as compared to eleven times each for the Poet and the Drunken Man, all of which fell in the 1748–49 season. He played Lord Chalkstone forty-eight times over twelve seasons. (See Appendix F of Leigh Woods, "David Garrick and the Actor's Means: A Revolution in Acting-Style, in Relation to the Life of the Times" [Ph.D. dissertation, University of California, Berkeley, 1979], pp. 393–95).

14. *The Plays of David Garrick*, ed. Harry William Pedicord and Fredrick Louis Bergmann (Carbondale: Southern Illinois University Press, 1980), I, 247–51.

15. The "father" roles which Garrick undertook after playing Heartly were: Zamti in *The Orphan of China* by Arthur Murphy; Aemilius in *The Siege of Aquileia* by John Home; Sir Harry Gubbin in *The Tender Husband* by Richard Steele; Oakly in *The Jealous Wife* by George Colman; Sir John Dorilant in *The School for Lovers* by William Whitehead; the Farmer in Garrick's own *The Farmer's Return from London*; Don Alonzo in *Elvira* by David Mallet; and Sciolto in *The Fair Penitent* by

Nicholas Rowe. The superannuated suitor was Sir Anthony Branville in Mrs. Frances Sheridan's *The Discovery*.

16. Elizabeth P. Stein has noted that *The Guardian* "is an excellent translation with some very slight textual changes of Barthélemi-Christophe Fagan's (1702–55) *La Pupille* (1734)." (See Stein's *David Garrick, Dramatist*, [New York: Modern Language Association of America, 1938], p. 87.) Even though Heartly was not an entirely original conception, Garrick selected the play and his role in it from a collection of dramatic works in his library which was considered during his lifetime to be the largest in the British Isles. The success and repetition of the Heartly-type in other plays demonstrates that the role had broad popular appeal, as well as its apparent personal appeal to Garrick himself.

17. Murphy, *The Life of David Garrick*, I, 28–30.

18. Margaret Barton, *Garrick* (London: Faber and Faber, 1949), p. 161; Oman, *David Garrick*, p. 222.

19. Percy Fitzgerald, *The Life of David Garrick*, rev. ed. (London: Simpkin, Marshall, Hamilton, Kent & Co., Ltd., 1899), p. 218.

20. *Lichtenberg's Visits to England*, trans. and ed. Margaret L. Mare and W. H. Quarrell (Oxford: The Clarendon Press, 1938), p. 10.

21. *The Letters of David Garrick* II, 635.

22. In two letters to Jean-Baptiste Suard, Garrick promised to read Diderot's *Paradoxe sur le comédien* and to send along to Suard his criticism of it. (See *The Letters of David Garrick*, II, 887–88; III, 1078.) Garrick never fulfilled his promises, even though he had met Diderot during his travels in France. Garrick's familiar reference to the essay of "our friend M. Diderot" in his second letter to Suard on the subject, written nearly three years after he had first received the manuscript, would seem either to constitute an embarrassed attempt at ingratiation of Suard after so long a delay or to signal his awareness of Diderot's interest in his reaction to the text of *Paradoxe*.

23. Denis Diderot, *The Paradox of Acting*, ed. Lee Strasberg (New York: Hill and Wang, 1957), p. 48.

24. See note 22.

25. Frederick Reynolds, *Life and Times*, I, 88–89; cited in Arthur Colby Sprague's *Shakespeare and the Actors: The Stage Business in His Plays (1660–1905)* (Cambridge: Harvard University Press, 1944), p. 302. Joseph R. Roach, Jr., has discussed this device, and others among Garrick's bag of tricks, in "Garrick, the Ghost and the Machine," *Theatre Journal*, 34 (1982), 431–40. In the essay, Roach considers Garrick's acting as a practical extension of Cartesianism.

26. *The Letters of David Garrick*, II, 481, 859; III, 1052, 1053. See also Jean Georges Noverre, *Letters on Dancing and Ballet*, trans. Cyril

W. Beaumont (New York: Dance Horizons, Inc., 1966), pp. 83–84. Noverre's descriptions of Garrick's performance-day habits come from an earlier part of the actor's career, most likely in the mid–1750s, when Noverre spent an extended period in London preparing his ill-fated "The Chinese Festival" for presentation at Drury Lane.

27. Writing in the November 2–4, 1773, issue of the *St. James's Chronicle*, "Eumenes" chastened one letter writer for having criticized a bit of business in Garrick's Macbeth: "The Gentleman has surely not seen Mr. Garrick act Macbeth these ten Years, else he could not have charged him with breaking a truncheon upon a Messenger's Arm. . . . In his late Representation of the Character, when the Messenger informed him of the Marching of Birnam Wood, he put his Hand upon his Sword, and, with a Look of Terror mixed with Dispondency [*sic*], pronounced his threat to him" (cited in Arthur Colby Sprague, *Shakespeare and the Actors*, pp. 275–76). In a letter dated January 10, 1773, and having played the role over nearly thirty years, Garrick stated his intention to play Macbeth "in the old Dress with New Scenes" (*The Letters of David Garrick*, II, 846), a plan which, for some reason, he did not carry out. He performed his last Macbeth in the fall of 1768. Finally, Georg Lichtenberg testified that, having been unsatisfied with Garrick's reading of Hamlet's "smile and smile and be a villain" the first time he had seen Garrick perform it, he was "gratified and charmed to hear him declaim the same words in a manner entirely in accord with my own sentiments, namely, in the purposeful tone of one bent on immediate action" (*Lichtenberg's Visits to England*, pp. 30–31). Garrick's apparent change in reading, in a role he had played for over thirty years, came in the 1774–75 season, his next-to-last on the stage.

28. See Appendix D of Woods, "David Garrick and the Actor's Means," p. 386.

29. Garrick, *Essay*, p. 4.

6

The Actor as Trickster: Illusionism on the Eighteenth-Century English Stage

Acting is always composed in equal parts of truth and illusion, and Garrick's acting dealt in these quantities, too. To the degree that he exploited new definitions of the natural, he obliged himself to tap new varieties of artifice. If the majority of his viewers were caught up in the realistic surfaces of his acting, his critics often preoccupied themselves with searching out the technique behind the appearance. Garrick, like any great actor, was challenged continually to adapt his methods so as to disguise them as "nature" or to make them invisible altogether.

The greatest illusion constructed by Garrick's skill as an actor lay in the notion that the workings of sympathy and sentiment exhausted the range of human concern. This chapter attempts to measure the "reality" of Garrick's stage in terms of what it ignored or sidestepped, as well as in what it featured. To some extent Garrick seems to have absorbed the limitations of his age by acting so eagerly and so often as its apologist. But the age also reflected his limitations in its willingness to applaud him as the epitome of its values. We shall now look more closely at these personal limitations, and at their implications about areas left unresolved or rendered unpleasant by the assumptions of eighteenth-century life.

Time Leading Garrick Away from Comedy and Tragedy, by Robert Laurie after T. Parkinson. Reproduced by permission of the Trustees of the British Museum.

MIMICRY OR SINCERITY?

One of Garrick's distinctions as an actor came in his ability to reconcile a striking gift for mimicry with a technique which made his characterizations appear whole and startlingly new. His success at integrating mimicry into psychologically coherent and sympathetically conceived characterizations stands as a distinctive feature of his acting, separating it from the emotionally raw and exhausting performances of his foremost Romantic successors, Siddons, Kemble, and Kean, and from the sterile and narrow characterizations of the pure mimics of his own time, like Samuel Foote. His sympathetic approach to character also marked Garrick off from the more judgmental style refined on Restoration stages, and his resort to life studies as a source for both conception and execution endowed his acting with a playfulness and flexibility essentially lacking in the Romantic actors, who drew regularly on areas of the subjective and hypothetical in their approach to dramatic character.[1] This joining of the mimetic to the sympathetic in Garrick's style may go far toward explaining his versatility, matched only by Richard Burbage, apparently, among his predecessors and by Laurence Olivier among his successors. For Garrick, indeed, mimicry may have stood as a physical expression of sympathy.

But it did not stand with him, as it did with Colley Cibber, as one of the most valuable expressive skills in the actor's repertoire. Cibber had boasted of his own strict imitations of Sandford and Dogget in his characterizations of Richard III and Fondlewife in Congreve's *The Old Batchelor*, respectively. He cited these imitations, in fact, as proof of his early distinction as an actor:

At my first appearance, one might have imagin'd, by the various Murmurs of the Audience, that they were in doubt whether Dogget himself were not return'd, or that they could not conceive what strange Face it could be, that so nearly resembled him; for I had laid the Tint of forty Years, more than my real Age, upon my Features, and, to the most minute placing of an Hair, was dressed exactly like him: when I spoke, the Surprize was still greater, as if I had not only borrowed his Cloaths, but his Voice too.[2]

Garrick, by way of contrast, never used imitation as a means for framing an entire character. He seems, rather, to have used it in more fleeting ways, and at times to some specific comic purpose, as in his performance of Bayes in an updated version of the Duke of Buckingham's *The Rehearsal*. In this characterization, which he introduced just beyond the halfway point of his first season, mimicry was enlisted in the name of proclaiming his independence of earlier styles of acting. According to Arthur Murphy, Garrick "seized the opportunity to make *the Rehearsal* a keen and powerful criticism on the absurd stile [*sic*] of acting that prevailed on the stage. . . . He selected some of the most eminent performers of the time, and, by his wonderful powers of mimicry, was able to assume the air, the manner, and the deportment of each in his turn."[3]

The "absurd stile" which Garrick chose to satirize while still in his first season on the stage was tragic acting in the form which it had assumed in the years immediately prior to his debut. His imitation of Dennis Delane, in particular, at the time the foremost tragedian aside from Quin, captured Delane's proud and idiosyncratic habit of placing his finger on the side of his nose when he spoke. Garrick's omission of Quin from his list of caricatures is curious,[4] but by refraining from ridiculing his most important rival Garrick may have been seeking to blunt the overtly aggressive edge of his challenge to the theatrical establishment, even as his writing and acting of Sharp in *The Lying Valet* had sought to do some two months previous.

Garrick's manner of playing Bayes also worked to distinguish him from the actors who had taken the role before him. As Thomas Davies noted,

The difference between Garrick and his immediate predecessors, was very conspicuous. They, by their action, told the spectators that they felt all the ridicule of the part; he appeared quite ignorant of the joke that made against him. They seemed to sneer, at the folly of Bayes, *with* the audience; the audience laughed loudly *at* him. By seeming to understand the satire, they laught at the approbation of the pit; he gained their loudest plaudits, without letting them know he deserved it. They were in jest; he was in earnest.[5]

As Bayes, then, Garrick chose to assume the audience's laughter and ridicule on himself—aside, perhaps, from the moments of his impersonations of the other actors—and his sympathetic identification with the character removed from it the element of "comment" prominent in the performances of earlier interpreters of the role. It is significant that two of Garrick's predecessors as Bayes were Colley and Theophilus Cibber (perhaps the unnamed "they" of Davies' comparison), who were among the leaders of the negative voices which greeted Garrick's acting in the aftermath of his stunning debut. These men showed acuity as critics, however, in their quick identification of Garrick as an actor whose approach to dramatic character, in comedy as well as in tragedy, challenged the fundamental assumptions of their own style.

In May 1742, at the end of his first season and three and one-half months after assuming the role, Garrick recreated his Bayes for his first appearance at the prestigious Drury Lane theater, and this event as much as any other signaled his accession to the ranks of respected and respectable actors. His move to Drury Lane permanently for the following (1742–43) season suggests his nearly immediate recognition as a commercial asset among London theater folk, and it also marks his achievement of a general level of acceptability among the more polite and refined audience which patronized the royal patent houses. His reward for joining the Drury Lane company for the 1742–43 season was a salary of £500, which stood at the time as the highest ever offered to an English actor.[6] Curiously, having once established his ascendancy, Garrick appears to have turned suddenly away from the personal caricatures which had sprinkled his characterization of Bayes.

Davies offers a partial explanation for this decision in his hypothesis that

Mr. Garrick now considered himself in a different situation from that in which he had hitherto been placed. As manager and actor of Goodman's Fields playhouse [the theater where Garrick had made his debut], he thought himself warranted to act with somewhat less caution, and to venture at bolder hazards, than when he found himself ranked as the principal actor in the King's theatre of Drury-lane.[7]

But Garrick's apparently conscious subordination of satirical mimicry in his acting was almost certainly related, too, to the growing opinion that "imitation," of which mimicry would have been considered a variety, involved the sacrifice of originality and sincerity. As the poet and essayist Edward Young put it in his "Conjectures on Original Composition" in 1759, "by a spirit of *Imitation* we counteract nature, and thwart her design."[8] This view coincides with the rising currency of the image of artistic genius, and with the spreading view that artists created not out of norms and rules but rather out of the synthesizing force of their own imaginations.[9] In any case, it appears that Garrick's subsequent playing of Bayes was directed away from explicit personal satire—communicated mainly through mimicry—and toward a more topical and literary kind of humor.[10]

Later in his career, Garrick seems never to have resorted to mimicry in the same way that he had with his early Bayes, but he did continue to play the role and even reshaped its depiction of the meddling man of theater to stand as surrogates for himself in two of his own plays. Both *A Peep behind the Curtain; or, The New Rehearsal* (1767) and *The Meeting of the Company; or, Bayes's Art of Acting* (1774) demonstrate once again Garrick's tendency to explain or to ingratiate himself through self-ridicule. Perhaps because he did not act in these plays himself, however, his literary hand felt freer to seek out deeper similarities between the Bayes-prototype of the meddler and his real self than had seemed prudent in the previous roles which he had written to play himself. As a group, too, the earlier list of Garrick's characters in his own plays lacked the frequent references to issues of power and authority which appear in the later two plays based on the rehearsal format. Instances of explicit self-mockery in these later plays, in literary terms at least, come much closer to the mark than they had in Garrick's earlier parodies of himself, which generally sidestepped issues of managing and concentrated instead on more narrow facets of his public image.

In *A Peep behind the Curtain*, Garrick drew an "acting Manager [named Patent], who scarce reached to my third button," in the words of one normal-sized audience member among its *dramatis personae*; and Patent's jealous response upon first meeting a handsome young man is that he "was much too tall for a hero."[11] A bit later Patent is so flattered by a playwright's request that he write a prologue that the playwright, seeing Patent's elated response, is quite certain that he "shall be able to do anything with him."[12] In *The Meeting of the Company*, Garrick created another actual "Bayes," whose main function is in the exposition of his theories of an overwrought and external style of acting which will take the stage by storm:

> Be in extremes in Buskin, or in Sock,
> In Action Wild—in attitude a Block!
> From the Spectator's Eye, your faults to hide,
> Be either Whirlwind,—or be petrify'd. . . .
> To heighten Terror—be it wrong or right,

Be black your coat, your handkerchief be white,
Thus pull your hair to add to your distress,
What your face cannot, let your Wig Express.[13]

These lines capture, in caricatured form, the salient features of
Garrick's own style, with its extremes of motion and stillness, its
depiction of high passions and vulnerable states, and its occasional resort to tricks such as Hamlet's whirled handkerchief and
his mechanical wig. There is a sort of security in Garrick's willingness to mock himself in 1774 not evident in his *An Essay on
Acting* written thirty years before. Indeed, he seems to be associating his acting, in these lines, with the more thoroughly ex-
ternalized approaches of the older declamatory actors—whose
very style he had ridiculed in his earliest characterizations of
Bayes.

Even if his sympathetic approach to dramatic character had
not become universal practice among actors, Garrick may have
felt toward the end of his career that its virtues were sufficiently clear to free him to adopt a more even-handed and conciliatory response than he might have earlier to the few critics
of his acting. A certain self-mimicking in his later writing seems
to have replaced the mimicry of others in his earliest acting, and
his later plays, in particular, demonstrate a self-awareness lacking in his earlier dramatized versions of "himself," tailored for
the public consumption. Certainly in *The Meeting of the Company*
his focus as a mimic has shifted from earlier attacks on other
actors to a species of attack on himself.

And yet, behind the hints of mellowing lies the remarkable
consistency of Garrick's attempts to hone the sharper edges of
his image to popular taste. Still, as in the *Essay*, the subject of
controversy, still at the center of events, Garrick uses the extremity of Bayes's ideas about acting as the excuse for denying
him any real influence over the conduct of the stage; and he
clearly intends his audience to view Bayes, in his pretentious-
ness and old-fashioned ideas of acting, as the symbol—albeit a
ridiculous one—for himself.

Garrick had first created Bayes as an actor when he worked
at Goodman's Fields, and he had built into the character in his
first season a critical stance which seems to have approximated

his own as an "outsider" in his relation to the theatrical establishment. The second and most lengthy stage of his Bayes-char-
acterization followed the progress of his acceptance and rise
through the hierarchy of the London patent theaters, and his
Bayes during this period seems to have affiliated itself more
closely with the inner workings of the theater through its focus
on respectable though at times controversial literary issues.
Garrick may have been trying, in this, to legitimize himself by
abandoning his earlier confrontational strategy and painting
himself in the role as a sort of insider, still ridiculous as Bayes
but implicated nevertheless in the workings of the popular and
commercial stage. Finally, in his own two later plays treating the
theater and its workings, Garrick chose the period of the height
of his influence to draw theater-men as ineffectual as the original Bayes had been as his means of denying the strength and
consistency of judgment which he was exercising more often than
ever in his conduct of the Drury Lane. Once again, Garrick seems
to have been mixing the appearance of self-revelation with a
measure of disguise. The plays which contain his Patent and his
own Bayes are about managers and managing, and they affirm,
by implication, that Garrick's exercise of power as a manager
was random, capricious, and ineffectual. Clearly this was a view
of himself which, like the earlier ones, was calculated to inspire
his audience to refute it, in its less favorable associations.

During the last eleven years of his career, Garrick played *The
Rehearsal*'s Bayes only five times in three seasons, and not at all
during his last three years on the stage.[14] Before this period, in
the late 1750s and early 1760s, he had performed the role at
least once in eight consecutive seasons. Of his eight most frequently performed roles, Bayes ranks fifth; but among this group
it was the least performed once he had ceased taking on new
roles. Perhaps he grew tired of it, or perhaps his audience did.
It may also be that the role in a play nearly a century old could
no longer adjust to the particular conditions of Garrick's status
in the theater.

At the end of *A Peep behind the Curtain*, Patent is vilified by
Lady Fuz for his unwitting role in the elopement of young Miss
Fuz with a young man who had pretended to be an actor in

order to gain access to her. In *The Meeting of the Company*, Garrick has his Bayes leave the theater in a huff at the end of the play when the company he has been attempting to instruct in acting either ignores or ridicules him. In his new surrogates, Garrick took on the issue of managing, but in typical fashion he denied these characters any lasting or ultimate power over the conduct of the stage and in the larger world. On the one hand, his mimicry of himself grew more in its awareness of and willingness to consider issues which lay at the core of his personality; but in another sense it denied the reality of his ambition even more resolutely and focused even more narrowly on his own personality.

The ways in which Garrick adapted his mimic-gift encapsulate the best and worst parts of him. In his use of models from real life in his characterizations, Garrick was using mimicry in anticipation of the invention of photography and of the documentary form, as a means of vivifying, preserving, and celebrating the experience of ordinary men. This was a generous impulse on Garrick's part, and a self-effacing one, too. But in its employment as part of his image-making, mimicry became another tool for propounding laundered and idealized versions of himself to his public. In his tendency to manufacture such versions, Garrick was typical of his age in its reluctance to acknowledge the positive features of ambition, the love of fame, and aggression. This reluctance—and the popular images of it—make more sense when measured against one of the most expansionistic and aggressive periods of British colonial history. As a small actor with wide connections in society, Garrick embodied energies and implications similar to those which influenced the conduct of the growing British empire during his lifetime.

Besides his possible association with broad and consistent values within his culture, Garrick could make himself into very different things before very different people. Both on the stage and away from it, the extreme changes which sometimes characterized his behavior fed a popular myth that he must have been more than one person. The attribution of nearly magical powers to him contributed to a standing in his society more rich and extensive than the simple qualities of his acting seem to have justified. We shall look next at some of the manifestations and implications of his hyperdeveloped transformational capacity.

THE INFANTILE AND THE ANTIC

Garrick's transformations, it seems, could fool even his closest friends. One story has him pretending to be ill in bed to Dr. Messenger Monsey, who had planned to see him play King Lear that night. Having convinced Monsey that his understudy looked remarkably like himself when arrayed in Lear's costume and makeup, Garrick had waited for Monsey to depart, rushed to the theater, acted Lear with his usual distinction, and then raced home and back into bed to greet Monsey and enjoy his astonished account of the understudy's excellence.[15] Another story, on the authority of Samuel Johnson, had a friend of the Garrick family seeing David perform the hangdog Abel Drugger early in the actor's career and then reporting back to Peter Garrick, "Well, by God, Mr. Garrick, though he be your brother, he is one of the shabbiest, meanest, most pitiful hounds I ever saw in the whole course of my life."[16] Even if these tales are apocryphal, they present an image of Garrick consistent with several authenticated stories which touch on his playfulness and his transformational capacity. "Playing" in its broadest sense, was a natural function of his personality, and acting for Garrick was equivalent to playing, even as was the use of the words in his time. As an actor, Garrick was an embodiment of the playful spirit which, according to Johan Huizinga, suffused all areas of eighteenth-century life:

On the cultural side we find the spirit of ambitious emulation everywhere, manifesting itself in clubs, secret societies, literary salons, artistic coteries, brotherhoods, circles and conventicles. Every conceivable interest or occupation becomes a focus for voluntary association. Natural history collections and curios are all the rage. This is not to say that these impulses were worthless; on the contrary, it was precisely the whole-hearted abandon to play, the *élan* of it, that made them immensely fruitful for culture. The play-spirit also imbued the literary and scientific controversies which formed so large a part of the higher occupations and amusements of the international elite that waged them.

The distinguished reading public for whom Fontenelle wrote his *Entretiens sur la pluralité des mondes* was perpetually dissolving and regrouping about some controversial point or other. The whole of 18th-century literature seems to consist of lay and play figures: abstractions, pallid allegories, vapid moralizings. That masterpiece of capricious wit, Pope's "Rape of the Lock," could only have been penned when it was.[17]

Not only did Garrick inhabit the play-world—in a double sense—of the eighteenth-century stage, but he manifested a clearly antic side in his own personality. In a letter to the Reverend John Hoadly, Garrick demonstrated an almost Shandean flippancy and dizziness, for the pleasure of one of his oldest and most trusted friends:

> Your Invitation to Old Alresford I most cordially Accept of, & the little-ingenious *Garrick* with the ingenious little *Hogarth*, will take the opportunity of the *plump Doctor's* [Messenger Monsey's] being with You, to get upon a Horse-block, mount a pair of Quadrupeds (or one if it carries double) & hie away to the Rev'd Rigdum Funnidos [Garrick's nickname for John Hoadly, and a character in Henry Carey's farce, *Chrononhotonthologos*] at ye aforesaid Old Alresford, there to be as Merry, facetious Mad & Nonsensical, as Liberty, Property & Old October can make Em! huzza! I shall Settle the whole Affair with yr Brother [Benjamin Hoadly] tomorrow and shall wait his Motions: I am in raptures at the Party! huzza again Boys! Shan't I come with my Doctor? Yes; he gives me the potions & the Motions? Shall I loose my Priest? my Sir John? no, he gives me the proverbs & the No verbs [from *Merry Wives of Windsor*, III.i]. My cares are over, & I must laugh with You: Your French Cook is safe & sound & shall come with Me; but pray let us have no Kickshaws: Nothing but laugh & plumb pudding for
>
> Yr Sincere Friend & merry humble Servant
> D: Garrick[18]

Garrick's random and rapid associations offer a hint of the imaginative freedom which must have characterized his acting, too. His writing style in this letter is almost breathless, and we notice once again Garrick's tendency to hold his place at the center of events while at the same time ingratiating himself through gentle but persistent self-deprecation ("the little-ingenious *Garrick*," or "mount a pair of Quadrupeds . . . or one if it carries double"). Even on such an emotionally charged occasion as his retirement from the stage Garrick was capable of recounting the event shortly afterwards with a wistful and deflating humor: "Such a Night as Monday last was never Seen!—Such clapping, Sighing, crying, roaring, &c &c &c—it is not to be described!—in short— it was as we could Wish, *et finis coronat Opus*—ye Bell rings— Exit Nonsense. . . ."[19]

Garrick was also fond of diminutives, owing perhaps to his own small stature. His habitual salutation to the actress Catherine Clive, for years the leading comedienne at Drury Lane, was "Clivy-Pivy."[20] He signed himself "Davy-Pavy" in a 1777 letter to Martha Hale, and at the age of sixty addressed her in turn as "Haly-Paly."[21] His childlike aspect is evident, occasionally, in less happy circumstances, as when he complained to his brother George about an unanticipated royal command to play Oakly in Colman's *The Jealous Wife*. After having not played the part for several years, Garrick was alarmed at the prospect and he fulminated at his brother in his reluctance to relearn the lines and in his petty irritations at the other actors in the company:

I am very much *flabbergasted* that my good king will see me in *Oakly* & the deuce is in *You*, for not sending me the Prompter's Book . . . pray let me have it as soon as possible, the part I mean—that was a slip—I must be a[t] London (which I'm sorry for) on Tuesday to run over my scenes on *Wednesday Morning*—I have not played Oakly these three Years—Sick—Sick—Sick—and Mrs. Pd [Pritchard, who played Mrs. Oakly] will make me Sicker—great Bubbies, Noddling head, & no teeth—O Sick—Sick—Spew . . . could I hope that Mr Ramus could get ye Jealous Wife put off—but that's impossible I must do it, I'd give 5 Guineas to have the Prompter's Book now—but that can't be—Sick— Sick—King John beshit—bouncing, strutting, Striding, straddling, thumping, grinning, Swaggering, Staggering all be shit—No Matter— the more turd, ye More Stink, I hold my Nose. . . .[22]

With his mention of "King John beshit" Garrick was expressing his displeasure at the enthusiastic reception which had greeted the production of *King John* starring William Powell, who had once been Garrick's protegé but who had since gone on to become something of a rival. As a small, attractive man, and as one who had enjoyed, first, his family's attentions and later, nearly universal popular praise, Garrick may have been more than a bit spoiled. In any case, the prospect of appearing at a disadvantage before the king inspired an extreme reaction in him, and there are no parallel instances of helpless anger or feelings of impotence in his preserved correspondence. This, the lone surviving example of scatological usage on Garrick's part, offers the reminder that the roots of his attraction to acting had lain in the sensation of being caressed. When the caressing ceased, and when he felt the danger of its turning into scorn or indifference—particularly before the king and at the hands of a rival—he was capable of childish rage expressed in a childish vocabulary. This incident may also make us wonder how Garrick was able to maintain his equanimity in the face of several more difficult situations, and apparently to channel very similar feelings into more genteel expressions, as with his advice to his "sick monkey" to clap any flurries of unfair criticism to his "tail."

Garrick reportedly loved the company of children, although he had none of his own.[23] Another of the manifestations of the childlike in his own personality was his inventiveness as a practical joker. One of his most renowned pranks involved his feigning drunkenness, in competition with the French comedian Préville, to see whose state could be more alarming to passersby. Garrick finally won the contest when Préville himself began to grow concerned for him and interrupted the game by moving to offer Garrick assistance.[24] The authenticity of this story is one of the few involving Garrick's prankish side which can be corroborated, in this case by his letter to the Frenchman in which Garrick recalls him as "mon cher Compagnon en ivresse."[25] Still another story has the two actors waiting in a carriage marked for Versailles, but whose driver refused to move until a total of six passengers entered the vehicle. Garrick had gotten out four times, addressed the driver each time in a different voice and with an altered gait, and had finally succeeded in convincing the man that he had six fares—at which point the entire "group" had headed off for Versailles![26]

The portrait which emerges from such stories—of Garrick's gift for mimicry, of his playfulness, of his social acuity—captures a man quickly able to mirror those with whom he came into contact and to incorporate these impressions into his acting through the exercise of sympathetic imagination. His flexible body and fecund imagination found valuable complement in a native mimetic talent; he had the tact to exercise this talent tastefully, and so apparently unconstrainedly in situations from his private life. Baron Grimm described the actor after having met him as "a perfect monkey, imitating every thing he sees; yet he always remains graceful."[27] Grimm's observation suggests the older neoclassical bias that mimicry was inherently degrading and Grimm's opinion that Garrick was somehow able to overcome this liability.

Garrick's personality fit him well for assuming and re-creating many of the behaviors to which his busy life exposed him. His reliance on techniques based in physical experience helped him to avoid the tortured and isolated quality which seems to have characterized much of Romantic acting in tragedy. His ability to see humor even in the most unpleasant and difficult situations gave him and his acting the appearance of indomitability. His anger, when he felt it, was directed at specific and accessible targets rather than at an unfeeling cosmos. Mimicry and humor, of course, work generally as social functions, the one in its need for models and the other in its need of an audience. All these features of Garrick's personality—and of his acting—qualified his art as a social, a socialized, and a socializing expression, at least at the beginning.

THE PRIEST OF SENSIBILITY

Even as Garrick's acting stressed and flattered the humanitarian components of contemporary English life, the society it was intended to please moved in time beyond its early sanctioning of his acting to the veneration of it. During Garrick's career, playgoing became an act often associated with religious worship, and this development goes hand in hand with the enlightened disapproval of religious intolerance and with the incursions of empirical science on traditional faith. The sacramental tone which characterizes many of the accounts of Garrick later in his career pays homage to that part of his acting which struck his audience as timeless in its appeal and spiritual in its nature. In this connection, Garrick's acting served an increasingly skeptical age as a surrogate for the more traditional varieties of spiritual experience.

James Boswell ventured into this spiritual realm with his description of attendance at one of Garrick's performances in the early 1760s:

I went to Drury Lane and saw Mr. Garrick play *King Lear*. So very high is his reputation, even after playing so long, that the pit was full in ten minutes after four, although the play did not begin till half an hour after six. I kept myself at a distance from all acquaintances, and got into a proper frame. Mr. Garrick gave me the most perfect satisfaction. I was fully moved, and I shed abundance of tears.[28]

Boswell here assesses the value of his attendance at the play in terms of the intensity of emotion Garrick's performance aroused in him. Especially characteristic of eighteenth-century sensibilities is the pleasure Boswell seems to find in copious weeping. Presumably, some of the audience around him shared his feelings, and the presence of that audience seems to have worked in Boswell's mind to confirm and authenticate the typicality of his response.

It seems odd, though, that Boswell should have felt the need for privacy as he prepared himself for the sublime rigors of the performance, an event broadly social both by tradition and by nature. Also odd is Boswell's very need for getting into "a proper frame." One can imagine Garrick's needing to prepare himself for the performance as Lear, but the growing extremity of the sentimental response among his audience seems to have exacted a progressively greater demand on that audience as well. This preparation was one which worked to admit only the events onstage and to rule out the "distractions" posed by the presence of a live audience. The social dimension of playgoing suffered, apparently, when it became the common assumption that all men shared the same capacity to feel, and it suffered even more when audience members began to experience deeply sentimental responses to what they saw on the stage. Such persons must have been tempted to retreat into the privacy of public anonymity in the theater; and they were moved to celebrate

Garrick in ever greater hyperbole for his ability to manifest those same feelings in public which many of them felt reluctant to display in full measure in the theater—and which the likely intrusions of reality prevented them from ever experiencing in fullness and sublimity in private life, either. In short, Garrick's act was a hard one to follow.

If Boswell's testimony is any indication, the eighteenth-century spectator felt a growing need to maintain his sense of privacy in the face of ever more persistent appeals to his feelings. Actors, too, in the more rigorous exploration of personal experience which the sympathetic approach to dramatic character implied, came to feel the need for greater physical distance betweeen themselves and their audience. The criticism of acting from the generation prior to Garrick's debut developed an attitude toward the audience as a potential distraction to the actor in his work, rather than its raison d'être. Writing in 1733, Aaron Hill cautioned a young actor that "whenever you can forget an audience, you will charm them."[29] More than twenty years before this, an article in the *Tatler*, written probably by Richard Steele, had stated that "it is impossible to act with grace, except the actor has forgot that he is before an audience. Till he has arrived at that, his motion, his air, his every step and gesture has something in them which discovers he is under a restraint. . . ."[30] Such opinions suggest the growing currency of a notion that the value of theatrical endeavor extended beyond its broad address and strict utility to the audience as a group, and toward a kind of privileged communication which took place between the actor, in his sympathetic approach to the character he played, and the individual spectator in his sympathetic identification with that character. There lies only one short step between this image of theatergoing and the closet drama of the English Romantic period, which shrank from actual production in its assumption of the degrading capacity of the mass audience. Garrick may at times have felt this way himself, but even in the wake of the Half Price Riots he had fled the Drury Lane only to enlist in the more far-flung theater of European cultured society. It was his almost invariable impulse to engage the audience and not to renounce it.

Restoration playhouses had been smaller and more intimate

than were eighteenth-century theaters; Restoration actors had used the forestage, the area of the stage closest to the larger part of the audience, as their main playing area; and the elegant coterie audience had sat, often in significant numbers, on the stage itself. Each of these arrangements in the Restoration theater buildings suggests an environment characterized by proximity and familiarity between actors and audience, and among the audience itself. This supports an image of the essentially social flavor of playgoing during that age. Betterton's audience may not have approached social homogeneity, but it seems at least to have been aware of itself as a group.

Proximity and familiarity among actors and audience, however, was not equivalent to genuine social mobility for the Restoration players themselves; and unlike Garrick, Betterton never knew the luxury of being able to retire from the stage, trapped as he was by the combination of his own indigence in his later years and his society's rigid definition of what an actor ought to be. For the Restoration actor, his nearness to the audience served always to remind him of the aristocratic taste which sustained him in his profession and of the heroic ideal which had styled many of the characters he played. The closeness of the audience also reminded him that he was expected to share the stage and his part in the spectacle with the impulsive, lusty, and elegant set which allowed him to perform or prevented him from doing so, to be heard or not to be heard, as it wished.

In this way, the social mechanism of the Restoration playhouse reinforced the critical distance which prevailed between audiences of the time and the characters in the plays they watched. Restoration comedies, in particular, can be seen to embody this critical stance in their frequent use as platforms from which to launch personal attacks on particular members of the audience. The Duke of Buckingham's *The Rehearsal*, as we have seen, offers one of the more notable examples of such satire with its ridicule of John Dryden, in his incarnation as the pretentious and sable-garbed Bayes. Geoffrey Marshall has described the ways in which a formal critical distance between audience and dramatic characters was enforced by the assumptions of Restoration dramaturgy: "The audience to such a play is assumed to be educable, alert, critical, distanced, vain, and itself flawed. Each of these characteristics is necessary for a play with flawed characters to succeed in delighting and instructing the audience."[31] Dryden himself offers perhaps the clearest contemporary statement of the critical stance adopted by Restoration playwrights with his pronouncement that "the characters of comedy and tragedy . . . are never to be made perfect, but always to be drawn with some specks of frailty and deficience."[32] It may have been easier to see such specks from the Restoration audience's privileged positions on the stage or in the boxes than it was for the less proximate audience in the theaters of the later eighteenth century.

The flawed characters which populate the Restoration drama as Almanzors, Dorimants, Horners, and Antonys give way to the perfectible ones of the eighteenth century. From Colley Cibber's reformed rakes and Richard Steele's sober, feeling couples to the learning heroes and heroines of Goldsmith and Sheridan, dramatic characters ceased being drawn so as to sustain critical detachment in the audience and commenced to be captured in ways which were calculated to draw their audiences into sympathetic identification. Particularly after the passage of the Licensing Act in 1737, eighteenth-century audiences were increasingly encouraged to suspend their intellectual faculties in favor of their emotional ones and to view dramatic characters as the idealized reflections of their own experience. The tendency to consider dramatic characters primarily as moral entities demonstrates how sharply the assumptions about "personality" on Garrick's stage differed from those of the Restoration. The greater physical distance between Garrick's audience and its characters—which the actor himself enforced in 1762 with his final and complete removal of the audience from the stage—seems only to have fueled the collective tendency to see such characters as the embodiments of a kind of moral perfection which existed in potential form, at least, within the audience itself.

As Paul E. Parnell has observed, over the course of the eighteenth century the profusions of sentiment and of the idealized characters who experienced it worked to hypnotize playgoers and novel readers into the belief that dramatic and fictionalized characters were literal representations of goodness that existed in life, and to dispel any suspicions that a strict correspondence may not have existed between fictionalized worlds and the real one.[33] To the extent that Garrick perfected the surfaces of reality in prosecuting his sentimental aims as an actor, he may have been as guilty as anyone of fostering a kind of moral self-satisfaction among his viewers.[34] In the long run, sympathy and sentiment seem to have produced isolation and solipsism, rather than the engagement with the greater world and its problems which they appeared to promise in 1741, on the heels of Garrick's debut and the publication of Samuel Richardson's pioneering refinement of the novel-form, *Pamela*.

SYMPATHY AS ENGAGEMENT, AND SENTIMENTALITY AS WITHDRAWAL

A dynamic relationship between the communal and the personal components of theatergoing has always existed, and it seems to find a different point of balance in every age. This dynamic is also built into the nature of theatergoing, with its mixing of public and private experience and its synthesizing of these in performance. During Garrick's career, this synthesis was forged in the gap which existed between the increasingly verisimilar actions characters performed onstage and the aura lent to them by sheer distance, by more elaborate lighting, and by ever more detailed and lavish settings.

This synthesis, together with the tension it embodied, derived from the period's understanding of sympathy as the process by which man perceived himself in relation to other men. On the one hand, "sympathy" was used to describe the imaginative act of identification between one person and another and so was, by its very definition, a capacity exercised in a social context. But by making "sympathy" a subjective and voluntary activity, as did philosophers later in the century, the period began to root the origins of sympathetic response with more certainty in private experience. The older view that sympathy was involuntary had been propounded by Francis Hutcheson and others, and its implication was that all of humankind stood as a single, undifferentiated, "feeling" mass. But such views were replaced by the notion that education, or breeding, or some inborn distinction qualified some for extraordinary degrees of sympathetic identification, and this view led to the elitism and the cult of sensibility we examined earlier.[35]

Because art was seen as the most compelling and refined stimulus toward concentrated sympathetic feeling, the age moved increasingly, and largely unawares, toward an image of the sympathetic man as sufficient unto himself and capable of re-creating all human experience within the confines of his own imagination, having once observed its workings on the stage or in the world. For an audience member toward the end of Garrick's career, the experiencing of deep emotion in the concert-hall, the gallery, the theater, or the study seems to have become a self-contained and self-fulfilling event. A person could demonstrate his distinction as a human being in the sheer intensity of his sympathetic response to some figure in a work of art, rather than in the more active demonstrations of his sympathy as they might find outlet in the larger world.

This may help to explain why the playwriting of Garrick's time did not address itself in any significant way to the suffering experienced by large numbers of people in the displaced rural working classes, visible in London particularly as the urban poor. It may help to explain also why characters with menial occupations were persistently maintained as stock comic types. Such characters still stood to some extent as food for laughter, Garrick's altered creative assumptions in his rendering of them notwithstanding. The workings of eighteenth-century sympathy, in its progressive association with sentiment, dispelled deeper questions pertaining to social inequities, and they acted to fuel the middle class's sense of its own moral unassailability. The morally idealized characters which filled the domestic and sentimental plays written during Garrick's tenure on the stage conditioned the middle class, in particular, to seeing its own essential goodness reflected in dramatic heroes, and they stopped its members short of examining the darker implications of their own relatively recently improved standing and larger numbers.

In 1741, at the time of his debut, Garrick's acting represented a potentially powerful motive toward socially corrective impulses. Garrick's own untroubled middle-class aspirations and his acceptance of prevailing mixtures of sympathy and senti-

ment worked over the course of the next thirty-five years to deflect this initially revolutionary edge. It is unfair, of course, to
judge Garrick's acting primarily as a political quantity, and to
hold him responsible for the abuses and negligence in contemporary British political life. But it is instructive to see the same
capitalist energy which animated his conduct of the Drury Lane
theater at work in his acquisition of five thousand shares of stock
in the East India Company. It was this financial interest which
aroused his disapproval of the Boston Tea Party in the form of
his wish in 1774 to "make ye Bostonians drink their tea as they
ought, or send them after ye tea into ye atlantic."[36]

Horace Walpole considered Garrick's acting, on his first exposure to it, to be socially as well as artistically subversive. Such
criticism diminished, as we have seen, only as Garrick was able
to gain broader trust and acceptance as a private citizen. His
conduct furnished him with respectability, and his art eased his
entrée into the highest levels of British society—but only, perhaps, because it was so orthodox and inoffensive in its political
implications as to seem apolitical. Arthur Murphy testified that
"Garrick's political principles . . . made no part of his conversation. General topics were more agreeable to his way of thinking."[37] Garrick may not have had much choice in this: During
the one hundred years before his debut, the theater had suffered two defeats in confrontations with political movements.
The first had come with the deposition of the masque- and
theater-loving Charles I and the subsequent repressions of the
Commonwealth during the 1640s and 1650s, and the second with
the passage of the Licensing Act in 1737, the same year that
Garrick came to live in London.

The dangers of an avowedly political theater were clear and
one of their manifestations at least was within Garrick's memory. The rewards of an apolitical or at least noncontroversial
theater were great. Particularly after he had gained some fame
and recognition, Garrick was almost certainly inspired to follow
the path of least resistance in choosing plays in which to exercise his talents. Nor were plays containing sharp social criticism
in any great abundance during Garrick's time on the stage, the
Licensing Act having rendered such plays unproducible and so
unprofitable. Garrick himself turned toward charitable activi-

ties as numerous as they were inoffensive. In his lifetime, he achieved a reputation for open-handed generosity to needy and deserving friends, and it was largely through his efforts that a fund for retired actors was established.[38]

Garrick's talents as an actor found their extension in the heartfelt but politically melioristic humanism of the time, rather than in any active campaigning through his public reputation or his private influence for social reform. The subversiveness some of his early critics had identified in his acting was absorbed into the benevolent, broadly humanitarian, and ideally apolitical definitions of art and the artist which the middle class evolved as it moved to consolidate its standing. Having broken down the esthetic foundation for class distinctions between comic and tragic characters, Garrick does not seem to have been interested in carrying this motive in his style any further. At the same time that he was withdrawing upstage and away from his audience, Garrick withdrew also from the highly charged political arena which the stage had often represented between 1660 and 1737.

On the other hand, Garrick's refusal to use his art for political purposes aided him in his ability to concentrate on areas of private, subjective, and emotionally intense experience which he discovered in his characters. It is certain that the apolitical climate of the stage served increasingly to focus popular interest on the qualities of domestic life and on sensations of the individual soul which, within the sentimental framwork, were considered paradoxically to be universal.

At the same time that Garrick's sentimentalized heroes were growing more accessible to the audience in their speaking, their way of moving, and their address to material reality, they were also drawing away from it to become moral icons. One influence balanced the other, and this balance created a dramatically fertile tension in the onstage realizations of figures which the eighteenth-century deemed heroic. The complementary impulses toward naturalism, on the one hand, and toward moral idealization, on the other, can also be viewed as the mechanism through which an audience could be reminded of its own moral perfectibility. An increasingly familiar surface of objects, gestures, and inflections onstage contributed to the growing sense that the hero's moral distinction was as immediate and accessible as were his casual stance and his easy manner. Even beyond the period's growing preference for self-scrutiny over individual activism, it may actually have equated the two in the assumption that moral improvement would somehow lead automatically to action, as it could be seen to do in Garrick's sentimental heroes, compressed and theatricalized as they were and dyed in the remnants of neoclassical dynamism.

Michael Goldman has written in *The Actor's Freedom* that "a culture's leading dramatic roles reflect its attitude to actors and acting, but even more they reflect its sense of where, outside the theater, terrific energies are likely to appear. The ambivalent energies aroused by theatergoing congregate in the person of the hero, and are released by the blasphemous/sacred freedom he pursues."[39] If Garrrick's mimicry and tendency toward a stricter behavioral authenticity in his acting represent the "blasphemous" side of Goldman's formula, his sentimental appeal and moral address will stand nicely for the "sacred" side. The illusion his acting helped to create for English audiences in the eighteenth century was made up of tensions so delicately balanced they could not long survive his passing from the stage. If the plays of the period have not survived in great numbers as living pieces for the stage, the sensibility which colored them has, in positive form through the writings of Stanislavsky on the practice of acting, and in negative form in the critiques of sympathetic assumptions in acting offered by Brecht and Artaud. Indeed, it may be that the attacks on the sympathetic depiction of dramatic character which have come in our own century have arisen out of the distaste of many for the superseriousness, hypersensitivity, and self-indulgence which have attached themselves to its modern practice. Such excesses have followed as the logical consequence of Romantic alienation, and they have subjected the sympathetic approach to strains which Garrick, as thoroughly socialized and engaged as he was, felt only in his moments of deepest despair.

As much as any other actor, Garrick is responsible for the serious philosophical treatment of acting which originated with Diderot. Both in its theory, essentially fragmentary, and in its practice, more thoroughly documented by verbal accounts and paintings, Garrick's acting offered up lively and provocative images to those who watched it. As a historical model, even in its state of partial preservation, it has continued to influence acting theory and practice to the present day. In its own time its vividness was enforced by Garrick's own personality, which was a literally "expressive" one in its reach outward to his audience and to his world. That his audience increasingly reached back toward him, rather than out into the real world, is at once the greatest tribute to, and the greatest paradox of, his acting in its social dimension.

NOTES

1. Joseph Donohue, *Dramatic Character in the English Romantic Age* (Princeton: Princeton University Press, 1970), pp. 253–69, 313–43.

2. Colley Cibber, *An Apology for the Life of Mr. Colley Cibber* (London: Printed by John Watts for the Author, 1740), pp. 119–21.

3. Arthur Murphy, *The Life of David Garrick, Esq.* (London: J. F. Foot, 1801), I, 52–53.

4. The actors whom Garrick sent up were, besides Delane, Sacheverel Hale, Roger Bridgewater, and Lacy Ryan. See Carola Oman, *David Garrick* (Bungay, Suffolk: Hodder & Stoughton, 1958), p. 45; Murphy, *The Life of David Garrick*, I, 56.

5. Thomas Davies, *Dramatic Miscellanies* (London: Printed for the Author, 1784), III, 303–4.

6. Murphy, *The Life of David Garrick*, I, 41.

7. Davies, *Memoirs of the Life of David Garrick, Esq.* (London: Printed for the Author, 1780), I, 53.

8. Edward Young, "Conjectures on Original Composition," ed. Edith J. Morley (1759; rpt. London: Longmans, Green & Co., 1918), p. 19.

9. See William Duff, *An Essay on Original Genius* (1767; rpt. Gainesville, Fla.: Scholars' Facsimiles & Reprints, 1966); Alexander Gerard, *An Essay on Genius* (1774; rpt. Munich: Wilhelm Fink Verlag, 1966); and Paul Kaufman's "Heralds of Original Genius," in *Essays in Memory of Barrett Wendall* (Cambridge: Harvard University Press, 1926), for an early but cogent discussion of the eighteenth century's interest in the working of genius and the ways in which this interest refined itself.

10. James J. Lynch, *Box, Pit, and Gallery* (Berkeley: University of California Press, 1953), p. 42.

11. *The Plays of David Garrick*, ed. Harry William Pedicord and Fredrick Louis Bergmann (Carbondale: Southern Illinois University Press, 1980), II, 71.

12. *The Plays of David Garrick*, II, 85.

13. *The Plays of David Garrick* II, 247–48.

14. See Leigh Woods, "David Garrick and the Actor's Means: A Revolution in Acting-Style, in Relation to the Life of the Times" (Ph.D. dissertation, University of California, Berkeley, 1979), p. 392.

15. Oman, *David Garrick*, p. 222; George Winchester Stone, Jr., and George M. Kahrl, *David Garrick: A Critical Biography* (Carbondale: Southern Illinois University Press, 1979), p. 118.

16. Percy Fitzgerald, *The Life of David Garrick*, rev. ed. (London: Simpkin, Marshall, Hamilton, Kent & Co., Ltd., 1899), p. 272n.

17. Johan Huizinga, *Homo Ludens: A Study of the Play-Element in Culture* (Boston: Beacon Press, 1955), p. 187.

18. *The Letters of David Garrick*, ed. David M. Little and George M. Kahrl (Cambridge: Harvard University Press, 1963), I, 78–79.

19. *The Letters of David Garrick*, III, 1108.

20. *The Letters of David Garrick*, III, 950.

21. *The Letters of David Garrick*, III, 1176.

22. *The Letters of David Garrick*, II, 556–57.

23. Margaret Barton, *Garrick* (London: Faber and Faber, 1949), pp. 256–59.

24. Oman, *David Garrick*, p. 252.

25. *The Letters of David Garrick*, III, 978. Translated: "My dear companion in drunkenness . . . "

26. Oman, *David Garrick*, p. 253.

27. From Grimm's *Correspondence littéraire* (1765), V, 318; cited in Frank A. Hedgcock, *A Cosmopolitan Actor: David Garrick and His French Friends* (London: Stanley Paul & Co., 1911), p. 234.

28. James Boswell, *Boswell's London Journal, 1762–1763*, ed. Frederick A. Pottle (New York: McGraw-Hill Book Company, Inc., 1950), pp. 256–57.

29. Aaron Hill, *The Works of the Late Aaron Hill* (London: Printed for the Benefit of the Family, 1753), I, 156.

30. *The Tatler*, no. 138 (February 1710), ed. George A. Aitken, vol. III (1898–99; rpt. Hildesheim: Georg Olms Verlag, 1970), p. 130. Steele put this thought in the mouth of Charles Hart, the great Restoration actor and major rival to Betterton until his retirement in the early 1680s and his death in 1683. Steele was only eleven years old when Hart died, and so it is likely either that he was repeating Hart's thoughts as hearsay or that he was looking to legitimize the notion of an actor's obliviousness to the audience by ascribing it to Hart himself—who was in no position to refute the view. Even if the idea that actors were better off maintaining their concentration exclusive of the audience had been originated, or subscribed to, by Hart, it is significant that the view did

152   Garrick Claims the Stage

not gain any wider currency until after the turn of the eighteenth century.

31. Geoffrey Marshall, *Restoration Serious Drama* (Norman: University of Oklahoma Press, 1975), p. 192.

32. John Dryden, "Parallel of Poetry and Painting," *Critical Essays*, II, 184; cited in Marshall, *Restoration Serious Drama*, p. 190.

33. Paul E. Parnell, "The Sentimental Mask," *PMLA*, LXXVIII (1963), 529–35.

34. Lynch, *Box, Pit, and Gallery*, p. 246.

35. The evolution in the meaning given to "sympathy" has been discussed by John B. Radner in "The Art of Sympathy in Eighteenth-Century British Moral Thought," *Studies in Eighteenth-Century Culture*, vol. 9, ed. Roseann Runte (Madison: University of Wisconsin Press, 1979), pp. 193–94.

36. *The Letters of David Garrick*, III, 920.

37. Murphy, *The Life of David Garrick*, II, 198.

38. Fitzgerald, *The Life of David Garrick* p. 445; *The Letters of David Garrick*, III, 934, n. 2.

39. Michael Goldman, *The Actor's Freedom: Toward a Theory of Drama* (New York: The Viking Press, 1975), p. 56.

Appendix:
Garrick's Roles

Garrick's roles are listed here in the order in which the plays which contain them appeared in their original forms. The dates of Shakespeare's plays are taken from *The Folger Guide to Shakespeare*, ed. Louis B. Wright and Virginia A. LaMar (New York: Washington Square Press, 1969); and the dates of Garrick's adaptations and alterations are drawn from *The Plays of David Garrick*, ed. Harry William Pedicord and Fredrick Louis Bergmann (Carbondale: Southern Illinois University Press, 1980–82).

Role (Play)	Date Written
1 Richard III	1592–93
2 Romeo—adapted by Garrick in 1748	1594–95
3 Mercutio	1594–95
4 King John	1596–97
5 Faulconbridge (*King John*)	1596–97
6 Hotspur (*1 Henry IV*)	1597–98
7 King (*2 Henry IV*)	1597–98
8 Kitely (*Every Man in His Humour*)— adapted by Garrick in 1751	1598
9 Chorus (*Henry V*)	1598–99
10 Benedick (*Much Ado about Nothing*)	1598–99
11 Hamlet—adapted by Garrick in 1772	1600–01

Role (Play)	Date Written
12 Ghost (*Hamlet*)	1600–01
13 Othello	1604–05
14 Iago	1604–05
15 King Lear—adapted by Garrick in 1756	1605–06
16 Macbeth—adapted by Garrick in 1744	1605–06
17 Antony (*Antony and Cleopatra*)—adapted by Garrick in 1759	1606–07
18 Posthumus (*Cymbeline*)—adapted by Garrick in 1761	1609–10
19 Abel Drugger (*The Alchemist*)—adapted by Garrick in 1743	1610
20 Leontes (*The Winter's Tale*)—adapted by Garrick into *Florizel and Perdita* in 1756	1610–11
21 Don John (*The Chances*—John Fletcher)—adapted by Garrick in 1754	1613–25
22 Leon (*Rule a Wife and Have a Wife*—John Fletcher)—adapted by Garrick in 1756	1624
23 Wilding (*The Gamester*—James Shirley)—adapted by Garrick into *The Gamesters* in 1757	1633
24 Bayes (*The Rehearsal*—George Villiers)—adapted by Garrick in 1742	1671
25 Chamont (*The Orphan*—Thomas Otway)	1680
26 Pierre (*Venice Preserved*—Thomas Otway)	1682
27 Jaffier (*Venice Preserved*)	1682
28 Fondlewife (*The Old Batchelor*—William Congreve)	1693
29 Biron (*The Fatal Marriage*—Thomas Southerne)—adapted by Garrick into *Isabella* in 1757	1694
30 Aboan (*Oroonoko*—Thomas Southerne)	1696

Role (Play)	Date Written
31 Oroonoko (*Oroonoko*)	1696
32 Loveless (*Love's Last Shift*—Colley Cibber)	1696
33 Sir John Brute (*The Provoked Wife*—Sir John Vanbrugh)—adapted by Garrick in 1744	1697
34 Osmyn (*The Mourning Bride*—William Congreve)	1697
35 Sir Harry Wildair (*The Constant Couple*—George Farquhar)	1699
36 Clodio (*Love Makes a Man*—Colley Cibber)	1700
37 Witwoud (*The Way of the World*—William Congreve)	1701
38 Duretete (*The Inconstant*—George Farquhar)	1701
39 Master Johnny (*The School Boy*—Colley Cibber)	1702
40 Lothario (*The Fair Penitent*—Nicholas Rowe)	1703
41 Sciolto (*The Fair Penitent*)	1703
42 Lord Foppington (*The Careless Husband*—Colley Cibber)	1704
43 Sir Harry Gubbin (*The Tender Husband*—Richard Steele)	1705
44 Don Carlos (*The Mistake*—Sir John Vanbrugh)	1705
45 Brazen (*The Recruiting Officer*—George Farquhar)	1706
46 Costar Pearmain (*The Recruiting Officer*)	1706
47 Plume (*The Recruiting Officer*)	1706
48 Archer (*The Beaux' Stratagem*—George Farquhar)	1707
49 Scrub (*The Beaux' Stratagem*)	1707
50 Marplot (*The Busy Body*—Mrs. Susannah Centlivre)	1709

Role (Play)	Date Written
51 Orestes (*The Distrest Mother*—Ambrose Philips)	1712
52 Hastings (*Jane Shore*—Nicholas Rowe)	1713
53 Don Felix (*The Wonder*—Mrs. Susannah Centlivre)	1714
54 Lord Townly (*The Provoked Husband*—Vanbrugh-Cibber)	1728
55 Periander (*Eurydice*—David Mallet)	1731
56 Gregory (*The Mock Doctor*—Henry Fielding)	1732
57 Lusignan (*Zara*—Aaron Hill)— adapted by Garrick in 1754	1735
58 Alfred (*Alfred, A Masque*—David Mallet and James Thomson)—adapted by Garrick in 1751	1740
59 Poet (*Lethe*—David Garrick)	1740
60 Drunken Man (*Lethe*)	1740
61 Frenchman (*Lethe*)	1740
62 Sharp (*The Lying Valet*—David Garrick)	1741
63 Jack Smatter (*Pamela*—James Dance)	1742
64 Millamour (*The Wedding Day*—Henry Fielding)	1743
65 Regulus (*Regulus*—William Havard)	1744
66 Zaphna (*Mahomet*—J. Miller and J. Hoadly)	1744
67 Tancred (*Tancred and Sigismunda*—James Thomson)	1745
68 Fribble (*Miss in Her Teens*—David Garrick)	1747
69 Ranger (*The Suspicious Husband*—Benjamin Hoadly)	1747
70 Young Belmont (*The Foundling*—Edward Moore)	1747
71 Demetrius (*Irene*—Samuel Johnson)	1749

Role (Play)	Date Written
72 Eumenes/Dorilas (*Merope*—Aaron Hill)	1749
73 Edward (Edward *The Black Prince*—William Shirley)	1750
74 Horatius (*The Roman Father*—William Whitehead)—altered by Garrick for premiere	1750
75 Gil Blas (*Gil Blas*—Edward Moore)	1751
76 Mercour (*Eugenia*—Philip Francis)	1752
77 Beverley (*The Gamester*—Edward Moore)	1753
78 Demetrius (*The Brothers*—Edward Young)	1753
79 Dumnorix (*Boadicea*—Richard Glover)	1753
80 Virginius (*Virginia*—Henry Crisp)	1754
81 Aletes (*Creusa*—William Whitehead)	1754
82 Achmet (*Barbarossa*—John Brown)	1754
83 Athelstan (*Athelstan*—John Brown)	1756
84 Lord Chalkstone (*Lethe*—David Garrick)—altered by Garrick in 1756	1756
85 Lysander (*Agis*—John Home)	1758
86 Pamphlet (*The Upholsterer*—Arthur Murphy)	1758
87 Heartly (*The Guardian*—David Garrick)	1759
88 Zamti (*The Orphan of China*—Arthur Murphy)	1759
89 Lovemore (*The Way to Keep Him*—Arthur Murphy)	1760
90 Aemilius (*The Siege of Aquileia*—John Home)	1760
91 Oakly (*The Jealous Wife*—George Colman)	1761
92 Sir John Dorilant (*The School for Lovers*—William Whitehead)	1762
93 Farmer (*The Farmer's Return from London*—David Garrick)	1762

Role (Play)	Date Written
94 Don Alonzo (*Elvira*—David Mallet)	1762
95 Sir Anthony Branville (*The Discovery*—Mrs. Frances Sheridan)	1763
96 "Ode to the Memory of Shakespeare" (David Garrick)	1769

Bibliographical Essay

The notes to each chapter provide full citations for many of the sources which have informed the major divisions of this study. What follows here will try to guide readers to those materials that have offered me the most helpful and provocative views of Garrick and his life, or that treat matters related to him and his career on the stage. Most of the sources cited here appear somewhere in the notes, but I have tried to organize them in such a way as to suggest something of my own approach to Garrick's life and his work. In the interest of brevity, this essay will not include listings of all the plays in which he acted. Those titles that appear in the text appear also in the index.

BIBLIOGRAPHIES AND MODELS FOR RESEARCH

Gerald M. Berkowitz has recently made the mass of materials surrounding Garrick somewhat more manageable with his *David Garrick: A Reference Guide* (Boston, 1980). With the exception of eighteenth-century theater criticism, which Berkowitz derogates as "rudimentary and not worth hunting down," the bibliography is thorough, and all of the most important entries, together with many of the lesser works, receive short descriptions. Berkowitz has chosen not to duplicate the material contained in Mary E. Knapp, *A Checklist of Verse by David Garrick* (Charlottesville, 1955), or the glut of eighteenth-century biographies, memoirs, and novels which made some passing mention of the actor. Very thorough altogether, and especially so on continental sources

treating Garrick's career, is the critical bibliography contained in Michel
Perrin's dissertation, "David Garrick, Homme de Théâtre" (University
of Paris, 1976). The notes to George Winchester Stone, Jr., and George
M. Kahrl, *David Garrick: A Critical Biography* (Carbondale, 1979), are
massive and impressive in the breadth of sources to which they refer,
but the authors have chosen not to include a bibliography in their study.
As a listing of sources in philosophy, esthetics, and literary criticism
which bear on Garrick and his endeavor, the bibliographical essay contained in Joseph Donohue, *Dramatic Character in the English Romantic
Age* (Princeton, 1970), is very useful, and Donohue's entire approach
to researching the background of an actor's style stands as a model for
future studies.

Another book central to my thinking does not treat Garrick in any
specific way at all; but Michael Goldman, *The Actor's Freedom: Toward a
Theory of Drama* (New York, 1975), suggests a scholarly approach to
actors which lets them stand as indexes to larger values of the cultures
that applaud their work on the stage. Indeed, the germ of this volume
lies in Goldman's notion that actors stand often for larger values at
work within their societies.

BIOGRAPHIES AND CORRESPONDENCE OF GARRICK

There are a number of biographies with Garrick as their subject, and
I shall break these down according to the dates of their publication for
the convenience of the general reader. The first two among them were
written by men of the theater who knew Garrick from the stage and
had worked with him there. In both Thomas Davies, *Memoirs of the Life
of David Garrick, Esq.* (London, 1780), and Arthur Murphy, *The Life of
David Garrick, Esq.* (London, 1801), the modern reader may be struck
by loose organizations, anecdotal styles, and the almost entire absence
of scholarly rigor. We must remind ourselves that the books were written primarily for sale, rather than for information. In any case, their
shortcomings are redeemed by the richness of their theatrical perspec-
tives. Both Davies and Murphy incorporated into their books something of their own stormy and uneven relationships with the great actor, and this occasional prickliness lends an air of striking immediacy
to their re-creations of Garrick's life. George Kearsley included "A Short
Account of the Life and Writings of David Garrick, Esq." in his edition
of *The Poetical Works of David Garrick, Esq.* (London, 1785) and tried in
it to legitimize Garrick's standing as an author and man of letters to
those still inclined to dismiss him as a mere actor.

James Boaden edited *The Private Correspondence of David Garrick* in 1831 (London) and included at its beginning a "Biographical Memoir" running to just over sixty pages, which concentrates much of its attention on the controversies in the actor's life. The two biographies of the later nineteenth century are, on the whole, less satisfying than those which came from Garrick's contemporaries or near-contemporaries. Their greater historical distance from the actor creates an unconscious expectation of greater scholarly rigor in many modern readers, and neither book succeeds in living up to this expectation. Joseph Knight, in his *David Garrick* (London, 1894), contributed a body of previously unedited letters which he found in The Forster Collection, but he falls frequently into the sort of hearty theatrical anecdotes which seem now outdated and of dubious veracity. Knight's account runs very similarly in its essentials to that of Percy Fitzgerald in his *The Life of David Garrick*, rev. ed. (London, 1899), the 1868 edition of which Knight admits using as his own model. Fitzgerald's edition recommends itself in its pioneering attempt to marshall performance statistics for Garrick's acting career, and as the most exhaustive biography of Garrick until the appearance of Stone and Kahrl's work in 1979. A problem for all of Garrick's biographers, from the eighteenth century to the twentieth, has been to separate the mythmaking from the man. There was something in Garrick's nearly absolute mutability on the stage which seems to have lent itself to tales which feel manufactured—but which have been dutifully passed along nevertheless, and have thereby acquired the authority born of repetition.

Mrs. Clement Parsons, *Garrick and His Circle* (New York, 1906), attempted a rather narrower canvas of the actor's life than either the Knight or Fitzgerald biography and Parsons's book seems the better for it. Because she did not feel obligated to include a continuous account of Garrick's life, and because her approach often is thematic rather than chronological, Parsons explores eighteenth-century documentary materials rather more thoroughly and thoughtfully than her immediate predecessors did. Frank Hedgcock, in *A Cosmopolitan Actor: David Garrick and His French Friends* (London, 1912), undertook a treatment of Garrick in some ways even narrower than Parsons's, following an initial brief biographical overview with discussions of the actor's two trips to France and of his rather extensive correspondence in French, or with French citizens. The book may prove useful to readers wishing to explore the impact Garrick's acting had on continental theater and which neoclassical esthetics may have had on his own style.

Margaret Barton, *Garrick*, and W. A. Darlington, *The Actor and His Audience*, both appeared in London in 1949. Chatty and engaging, Barton makes her most original contribution to Garrick studies in her exploration of the "low" component in Garrick's acting which derived from the pantomime. Darlington devotes two chapters to Garrick, one on "Garrick the Man" and another on "Garrick the Actor," but he maintains an essential separation between the two views which makes any assessment of the actor's entire life difficult. Carola Oman, *David Garrick* (Bungay, Suffolk, 1958), appeared some nine years after Barton's and Darlington's books and represents the most carefully researched and organized biography of Garrick to appear before Stone and Kahrl's. Oman makes Garrick's experience more manageable by dividing it into smaller segments of time, and she finds compelling issues within each of these segments to indicate the larger tendencies in Garrick's development and change.

David M. Little and George M. Kahrl, *The Letters of David Garrick* (Cambridge, Mass., 1963), made an invaluable contribution to Garrick studies. Indeed, in many ways it offers a less distorted picture, often in the nature of "warts and all," than do the biographies. In its first volume the editors include an introduction to Garrick's life which calls the reader's attention to themes which recur in a number of the letters. This introduction succeeds admirably in its general purpose, at the same time that it lets the letters themselves speak loudest, and for themselves.

A Biographical Dictionary of Actors . . . in London, 1660–1800 (Carbondale) appeared in its sixth volume, from "Garrick to Gyngell," in 1978. The joint editors, Philip H. Highfill, Jr., Kalman A. Burnim, and Edward A. Langhans, offer a balanced and succinct account of the actor. They offer also one of the most complete iconographies of Garrick and continue the impulse inaugurated by Little and Kahrl to deal with Garrick's less admirable qualities in a fair and unapologetic way. Helen R. Smith, *David Garrick, 1717–1779* (Hatfield, England, 1979), is subtitled "A Brief Account," and it joins the *Biographical Dictionary* and Stone and Kahrl's study, which appeared also in 1979, as one among several books observing the bicentennial of Garrick's death. Michel Perrin, "David Garrick, Homme de Théâtre," I have mentioned already, and the first of its four sections is devoted to a biographical treatment of the actor. One of its most striking features lies in its attempt to synthesize Garrick's personality, through the mass of information which documents it, into several central motives or tendencies.

In addition to the preceding works, there exist a number of shorter treatments of Garrick which deserve mention, if only briefly, for their novel approaches to the actor's life: Sybil Rosenfeld, "David Garrick and Private Theatricals," *Notes and Queries*, CLXXXI (1941), 230–31; Dougald MacMillan, "David Garrick, Manager: Notes on the Theatre as a Cultural Institution in England in the Eighteenth Century," *Stud-*

ies in Philology, XLV (1948), 630–46; Mary E. Knapp, "Garrick's Last Command Performance," in *The Age of Johnson: Essays Presented to Chauncey Brewster Tinker* (New Haven, 1949), pp. 61–71; V. S. Pritchett, "The Unfrogged Frenchman," *New Statesman*, LXVII (1964), 167–68; Gareth Lloyd-Evans, "Garrick and the 18th Century Theatre," *The Johnson Society Transactions* (December 1965), 17–25; and George M. Kahrl, "Garrick, Johnson, and Lichfield," *The New Rambler* (June 1966), 15–28.

As a supplement to *The Letters of David Garrick*, the reader may wish to consult Boaden, *The Private Correspondence of David Garrick*, for the information it offers about the people to whom Garrick wrote; and The Earl Spencer and Christopher Dobson, *The Letters of David Garrick and Georgiana Countess Spencer, 1759–1779* (Cambridge, Eng., 1960), for its inclusion of the only extant letters of Garrick not contained in Little and Kahrl's *Letters*. For those wishing to know the actor through some of his other writings, *The Plays of David Garrick*, ed. Harry William Pedicord and Fredrick Louis Bergmann (Carbondale, 1980–82), is now available in seven volumes. Taken either singly or as a whole, this corpus will nicely embellish the images of his life and his work which Garrick himself furnishes in his *An Essay on Acting* (London, 1744), in Kearsley's edition of his collected verse cited earlier, and in Garrick's two travel journals, available in modern edited versions as *The Diary of David Garrick, Being a record of his memorable trip to Paris in 1751*, ed. Ryllis Clair Alexander (New York, 1928) and *The Journal of David Garrick, Describing His Visit to France and Italy in 1763*, ed. George Winchester Stone, Jr. (New York, 1939).

The number of eighteenth-century memoirs and biographies which mention Garrick is large, and I shall include here only those which are the most extensive in their references to the actor: James Boswell, *The Life of Johnson*, ed. George Birkbeck Hill, rev. L. F. Powell (Oxford, 1934), and *Boswell's London Journal, 1762–1763*, ed. Frederick A. Pottle (New York, 1950); Samuel Johnson, *The Rambler*, no. 200, February 15, 1752, which contains Johnson's supposed allegory of himself and Garrick as Asper and Prospero, respectively; Joshua Reynolds, *Portraits: Character Sketches of Goldsmith, Johnson, and Garrick*, ed. Frederick W. Hilles (New York, 1952); William Roberts, *Memoirs of the Life and Correspondence of Mrs. Hannah More* (New York, 1837); William Cooke, *Memoirs of Charles Macklin, Comedian* (London, 1804); *The Yale Edition of Horace Walpole's Correspondence*, ed. W. S. Lewis et al. (New Haven, 1937–1980), in which mentions of Garrick are in the index contained in volume 26 of the forty-two-volume series; and Tate Wilkinson, *Memoirs of His Own Life* (York, 1790).

GARRICK'S ACTING AND RELATED ENGLISH
THEATER HISTORY

Garrick's acting is explored extensively in the following works by his contemporaries: Thomas Davies, *Dramatic Miscellanies* (London, 1784), which touches on Garrick's handling of Shakespearian roles by way of its larger interest in the plays as pieces for the stage; Francis Gentleman, *The Dramatic Censor* (London, 1770), which though like Davies's work focuses on the general virtues of plays as dramatic literature, also offers glimpses of Garrick's acting in roles drawn from late-seventeenth-century and early-eighteenth-century works; Samuel Foote, *A Treatise on the Passions* (London, 1747), which although not always complimentary to Garrick gives rather thorough accounts of several key moments from the actor's characterization of King Lear; John Hill, *The Actor: A Treatise on the Art of Playing* (London, 1750; rev. ed., 1755), containing general descriptions of Garrick's technique and more specific ones of its application in several of his most renowned portrayals early in his career; Jean Georges Noverre, *Letters on Dancing and Ballets*, trans. Cyril W. Beaumont (New York, 1966), which includes interesting discussions of Garrick's Macbeth and of his performance-day habits; the anonymous *The Theatrical Review* (London, 1763), which contains an illuminating discussion of Garrick's approach to stage-speaking; and last, *Lichtenberg's Visits to England*, trans. and ed. Margaret L. Mare and W. H. Quarrell (Oxford, 1938), which offers the most extensive and detailed accounts of Garrick's acting that we have. Lichtenberg's treatment of Garrick's famous "start" as Hamlet, at the moment when the prince first sees his father's ghost, has become part of theatrical lore, but the book also contains fine descriptions of Garrick as Archer in *The Beaux' Stratagem* and as Sir John Brute in *The Provoked Wife*, the most lavish which have survived of Garrick's style in comedy.

The reader interested in gathering the dates and other details of Garrick's appearances as an actor will want to consult Part 3 of *The London Stage, 1729–1747*, ed. Arthur H. Scouten (Carbondale, 1961), and Part 4, encompassing the years from 1747 to 1776, ed. George Winchester Stone, Jr. (Carbondale, 1962). Critical introductions to each of these periods appear in the first volume of each part, and they have been published as separate volumes at Carbondale in 1968. The *Index to "The London Stage," 1660–1800*, comp. Ben Ross Schneider, Jr. (Carbondale, 1979), is despite its occasional inaccuracies and omissions helpful in guiding the reader toward a comprehensive image of the performance-documentation on Garrick's career which *The London Stage* contains. *Actors on Acting*, ed. Toby Cole and Helen Krich Chinoy (New

York, 1970), offers a survey of the methods of some of the great actors at work before, during and after Garrick and provides as well a good bibliography of acting sources in the eighteenth century. Arthur Colby Sprague, *Shakespeare and the Actors: The Stage Business in His Plays (1660–1905)* (Cambridge, Mass., 1944), is useful as a catalogue of Garrick's cleverness in devising original stage activities, often with assistance from carefully chosen stage properties.

Critical and analytical treatments of eighteenth-century English theater can be found in James J. Lynch, *Box, Pit, and Gallery* (Berkeley, 1953), which still stands as one of the best works on the theater and drama of the period, and in more recent studies such as Cecil Price, *Theatre in the Age of Garrick* (Oxford, 1973); *The Eighteenth-Century English Stage*, ed. Kenneth Richards and Peter Thomson (London, 1972); Allardyce Nicoll, *The Garrick Stage*, ed. Sybil Rosenfeld (Manchester, 1980); and *The London Theatre World, 1660–1800*, ed. Robert D. Hume (Carbondale, 1980). George C. D. Odell, *Shakespeare from Betterton to Irving*, volume 1 (New York, 1966), contains a wealth of detail on staging practices in Garrick's time and in the periods before and just after his career. Shorter articles which touch on Garrick's broad relationship to the theater of his day are William Angus, "Actors and Audiences in Eighteenth-Century London," in *Studies in Speech and Drama in Honor of Alexander M. Drummond* (Ithaca, 1944), pp. 123–38; and Raymond Pentzell, "Garrick's Costuming," *Theatre Survey*, X (1969), 18–42.

Background in the late- and post-Restoration periods can best be drawn directly from two contemporary works, Charles Gildon, *The Life of Mr. Thomas Betterton* (London, 1710), and Colley Cibber, *An Apology for the Life of Mr. Colley Cibber* (London, 1740). Latter-day treatments of the acting and theatrical traditions which preceded Garrick can be found also in Leslie Hotson, *The Commonwealth and Restoration Stage* (Cambridge, Mass., 1928); John Harold Wilson, *All the King's Ladies: Actresses of the Restoration* (Chicago, 1958) and "Rant, Cant and Tone on the Restoration Stage," *Studies in Philology*, LII (1955), 592–98; Arthur Colby Sprague, "Did Betterton Chant?" *Theatre Notebook* I (1946), 54–55; A. G. H. Bachrach, "The Great Chain of Acting," *Neophilologus*, XXXIII (1949), 160–172; Judith Milhous, "An Annotated Census of Thomas Betterton's Roles, 1659–1710," *Theatre Notebook* XXIX (1975), 33–43, 85–94; and Alan T. McKenzie, "The Countenance You Show Me: Reading the Passions in the Eighteenth Century," *The Georgia Review*, XXXII (1978), 58–73.

The eyewitness accounts of Garrick's acting which I have listed earlier are nicely supplemented by several scholarly attempts to re-create Garrick's acting style, most notably those of Alan Downer in "Nature to Advantage Dressed: Eighteenth Century Acting," *PMLA* LVIII

(1943), 1002–37; of Stone and Kahrl in chapter 2 of their *David Garrick: A Critical Biography*, titled "Garrick and the Acting Tradition"; of Edwin Duerr in *The Length and Depth of Acting* (New York, 1962); and of Bertram Joseph in *The Tragic Actor* (London, 1959). None of these works seems to me to succeed entirely in presenting Garrick's acting as an aggregate of technique, interpretation, and design, and several of the shorter treatments come closer to offering the reader vivid and particular images of Garrick at his work on the stage. Among these are Joseph Donohue, *Dramatic Character in the English Romantic Age*, which explores the literary background and interpretive context behind Garrick's playing of Richard III and Macbeth; George Taylor, " 'The Just Delineation of the Passions': Theories of Acting in the Age of Garrick," in *The Eighteenth-Century English Stage* (London, 1972), which investigates the theoretical and philosophical assumptions which underlay Garrick's style; Earl Wasserman, "The Sympathetic Imagination in Eighteenth-Century Theories of Acting," *The Journal of English and German Philology*, LXVI (1947), 264–72, which explores a broader theoretical framework than does Taylor's essay; and two articles by George Winchester Stone, Jr., "Garrick's Production of King Lear: A Study in the Temper of the Eighteenth-Century Mind," *Studies in Philology* XLV (1948), 89–103, and "The God of his Idolatry: Garrick's Theory of Acting and Dramatic Composition with Especial Reference to Shakespeare," in *Joseph Quincy Adams Memorial Studies* ed. MacManaway, Dawson, Willoughby (Washington, D.C., 1948). Joseph Roach's article, "Garrick, the Ghost, and the Machine," *Theatre Journal*, 34 (1982), 431–40, makes an ingenious attempt to integrate Garrick's acting within the ready Enlightenment categories of rationalism and empiricism.

In Garrick's own time, interesting and comprehensive philosophical views of acting were developed by John Hill in *The Actor*, in his notion of the actor as synthesizer of passionate "fire" and muscular control; by James Boswell, who in parallel fashion discussed the actor as the possessor of "double feeling" in "On the Profession of a Player," *London Magazine*, XXXIX (1770), 397–98, 468–71, 513–17; and finally and most famously by Denis Diderot in *The Paradox of Acting*, trans. Walter Herries Pollock, intro. Lee Strasberg (New York, 1957).

SOCIAL AND INTELLECTUAL HISTORY

Works of the twentieth century that have approached the eighteenth in ways useful to those interested in theater and the role of an actor in his society are numerous. Ones I have looked at and found helpful are Basil Willey, *The Eighteenth Century Background: Studies on the Idea of Nature in the Thought of the Period* (Boston, 1940); Paul Kaufman, "The Heralds of Original Genius," in *Essays in Memory of Barrett Wendall* (Cambridge, Mass., 1926), which remains stimulating and fresh after more than a half century of subsequent research; Walter Jackson Bate, *From Classic to Romantic: Premises of Taste in Eighteenth-Century England* (New York, 1961); Ernest Tuveson, *The Imagination as a Means of Grace: Locke and the Aesthetics of Romanticism* (Berkeley, 1960); Charles Vereker, *Eighteenth-Century Optimism: A Study of the Interrelations of Moral and Social Theory in English and French Thought between 1689 and 1789* (Liverpool, 1967); and John O. Lyons, *The Invention of the Self: The Hinge of Consciousness in the Eighteenth Century* (Carbondale, 1978). Two works which deal more narrowly with esthetics in proximate relationship to the stage are Frederick C. Green, *Literary Ideas in Eighteenth Century France and England: A Critical Survey* (New York, 1966), and Wilbur Samuel Howell, *Eighteenth-Century British Logic and Rhetoric* (Princeton, 1971).

In Garrick's own time there emerged at least a handful of philosophers whose works seem to color or to bear on Garrick's work for the stage. The reader may wish to go directly to John Locke, rather than to his recent interpreters; and *An Essay concerning Human Understanding*, ed. Peter H. Nidditch (Oxford, 1975), seems among Locke's works to incorporate notions which would most directly influence actors. Having examined Earl Wasserman's sense of sympathetic mechanisms at work in eighteenth-century theories of acting, one may then wish to look at Anthony Ashley Cooper, Third Earl of Shaftesbury, *Characteristics of Men, Manners, Opinions, Times, etc.* (Gloucester, Mass., 1963). Francis Hutcheson, *An Essay on the Nature and Conduct of the Passions and Affections . . .* (3d ed., 1742; rpt. ed. Paul McReynolds, Gainesville, Fla., 1969), is a book we know Garrick to have had in his possession early in his career; and in Edmund Burke, *A Philosophical Enquiry into the Origin of Our Ideas of the Sublime and Beautiful*, ed. J. T. Boulton (Notre Dame, 1958), we have a very influential book on esthetics written by one of Garrick's friends. Contemporary discussions of the "original genius" which seems to have animated so much of Garrick's work for the stage are contained in William Duff, *An Essay on Original Genius* (1767; rpt., Gainesville, Fla., 1964), Alexander Gerard, *An Essay on Genius* (1774; rpt. Munich, 1966), and Edward Young, "Conjectures on Original Composition" (1759; rpt. London, 1918).

The reader who wants to examine the phenomenon of sentimentalism as it attaches to Garrick's career will probably wish to consult the standard full-length works on the subject: Ernest Bernbaum, *The Drama of Sensibility* (1915; rpt. Gloucester, Mass., 1958), and Arthur Sherbo, *English Sentimental Drama* (East Lansing, 1967). To these have been added Robert D. Hume's essay, "Goldsmith and Sheridan and the

168   Bibliographical Essay

Supposed Revolution of 'Laughing' Against 'Sentimental' Comedy," in *Studies in Change and Revolution: Aspects of English Intellectual History*, ed. Paul J. Korshin (Menston, Yorkshire, 1972), pp. 237–76, and Richard Bevis's study of *The Laughing Tradition: Stage Comedy in Garrick's Day* (Athens, Ga., 1980). Other valuable works on the subject include Paul Parnell, "The Sentimental Mask," *PMLA* LXXVIII (1963), 529–35; R. F. Brissenden, *Virtue in Distress: Studies in the Novel of Sentiment from Richardson to Sade* (New York, 1974), particularly chapter 2, " 'Sentimentalism': An Attempt at Definition," pp. 11–55, and Brissenden, " 'Sentiment': Some Uses of the Word in the Writings of David Hume," in *Studies in the Eighteenth Century*, vol. I, ed. Brissenden (Toronto, 1968), pp. 89–107; and G. S. Rousseau, "Nerves, Spirits, and Fibres: Towards Defining the Origins of Sensibility," in *Studies in the Eighteenth Century*, vol. III, ed. Brissenden and J. C. Eade (Toronto, 1976), pp. 137–57. Other interesting treatments of sentiment and sympathy appear in Northrop Frye, "Towards Defining an Age of Sensibility," in *Eighteenth-Century English Literature: Modern Essays in Criticism*, ed. James L. Clifford (London, 1959), pp. 311–18; Robert Gale Noyes, *The Neglected Muse: Restoration and English Tragedy in the Novel, 1740–1780* (Providence, 1958); Mark Schorer's durable essay, "Hugh Kelly: His Place in the Sentimental School," *Philological Quarterly*, XII (1933), 389–401; Arthur Friedman, "Aspects of Sentimentalism in Eighteenth-Century Literature," in *The Augustan Milieu: Essays Presented to Louis A. Landa*, ed. Miller et al. (Oxford, 1970), pp. 247–61; and John B. Radner, "The Art of Sympathy in Eighteenth-Century Moral Thought," in *Studies in Eighteenth-Century Culture*, vol. 9, ed. Roseann Runte (Madison, 1979), pp. 189–210. The scholarly proliferation of definitions of sentimentalism and of attempts to describe its manifestations suggests the elusiveness of the term and indicates also that issues which the word raises admit more easily of debate than they do of solution.

Works which treat sentimentalism as part of a broader and more variegated tradition include Robert D. Hume, *The Development of English Drama in the Late Seventeenth Century* (Oxford, 1976); Geoffrey Marshall, *Restoration Serious Drama* (Norman, Okla., 1975); *The Revels History of Drama in English*, vol. V, *1660–1750*, ed. John Loftis et al. (London, 1976); Allardyce Nicoll, *A History of English Drama*, vol. II, "Early Eighteenth Century Drama" (Cambridge, Eng., 1952), and vol. III, "Late Eighteenth Century Drama" (Cambridge, Eng., 1961); and Frederick S. Boas, *An Introduction to Eighteenth Century Drama, 1700–1780* (Oxford, 1953). More specialized studies of the literature of the period are Ian Watt, *The Rise of the Novel* (Berkeley, 1957); George C. Branam, "Eighteenth-Century Adaptations of Shakespearian Tragedy," University of California Publications, vol. 14 (Berkeley, 1956);

Charles Harold Gray, *Theatrical Criticism in London to 1795* (New York, 1931); John Loftis, *Comedy and Society from Congreve to Fielding* (Stanford, 1959) and *The Politics of Drama in Augustan England* (Oxford, 1963); and Jean B. Kern, *Dramatic Satire in the Age of Walpole* (Ames, Ia., 1976).

Garrick's plays have been examined as a group in Elizabeth P. Stein, *David Garrick, Dramatist* (New York, 1938). A number of essays which treat Garrick's relationships with other important literary figures in his time have appeared over the years. Among these are Dougald MacMillan, "David Garrick as Critic," *Studies in Philology*, XXI (1934), 69–83; George M. Kahrl, "The Influence of Shakespeare on Smollett," in *The Parrott Presentation Volume* (Princeton, 1935), pp. 399–420; Ronald Hafter, "Garrick and *Tristram Shandy*," *Studies in English Literature, 1500–1900*, VII (1967), 475–89; and Lewis M. Knapp, "Smollett and Garrick," in *Elizabethan Studies and Other Essays in Honor of George F. Reynolds* (Boulder, 1945), pp. 233–43.

Among broader treatments of eighteenth-century life, Johan Huizinga, *Homo Ludens: A Study of the Play-Element in Culture* (Boston, 1955), is particularly useful in suggesting forces at work in Garrick's time which lent themselves to the peculiar force of his personality. Two of John Loftis's books mentioned earlier, *Comedy and Society from Congreve to Fielding* and *The Politics of Drama in Augustan England*, succeed in evoking a sense of the stage as an institution which reflected larger social and political tensions in the period. George Rudé, *Paris and London in the Eighteenth Century: Studies in Popular Protest* (New York, 1952), stands as one of the pioneering efforts to uncover the darker and more ominous sides of eighteenth-century life. This attempt has been elaborated by, among others, Harry C. Payne and his essay, "Elite versus Popular Mentality in the Eighteenth Century," *Studies in Eighteenth-Century Culture*, vol. 8, ed. Roseann Runte (Madison, 1979), pp. 3–32. And Joan Wildeblood, *The Polite World: A Guide to the Deportment of the English in Former Times* (London, 1965), conjures up images of the social manners which formed the matrix for many of Garrick's innovations on the stage.

The most general and sweeping treatment of the role of children and child rearing in eighteenth-century English life is Lawrence Stone's landmark work, *The Family, Sex and Marriage in England, 1500–1800* (New York, 1977). The interested reader can supplement this massive study with shorter ones, such as J. H. Plumb, "The New World of Children in Eighteenth-Century England," *Past and Present*, 67 (1975), 64–95; Judith Laurence-Anderson, "Changing Affective Life in Eighteenth-Century England and Samuel Richardson's *Pamela*," in *Studies in Eighteenth-Century Culture*, vol. 4, ed. Harry C. Payne (Madison, 1981), pp. 445–56; Laura A. Curtis, "A Case Study of Defoe's Domestic Conduct Manuals Suggested by *The Family, Sex and Marriage in England, 1500–1800,*" also in *Studies in Eighteenth-Century Culture,* vol. 4, pp. 409–28; and Bogna W. Lorence, "Parents and Children in Eighteenth-Century Europe," *History of Childhood Quarterly,* II, no. 1 (1970), 1–30. Longer studies of family dynamics in Garrick's time are Edward Shorter, *The Making of the Modern Family* (New York, 1975), and Randolph Trumbach, *The Rise of the Egalitarian Family: Aristocratic Kinship in Domestic Relations in Eighteenth-Century England* (New York, 1978).

Index

46, 48–50; on the stage, 41–42, 48, 52–53, 144–45, 148–49; and subjectivity, 145–46
Shaftesbury, Anthony Ashley, third earl of, 7, 34
Shakespeare, William, 19, 39–40, 50, 53, 69, 71–72, 109. Works in which Garrick took roles: *Antony and Cleopatra*, 19, 22, 82; *Cymbeline*, 65; *Hamlet*, 22–24, 66, 71, 87, 119–20, 122, 126 n.27; *King John*, 34–36, 65; *King Lear*, 13, 35–36, 40–42, 51, 66, 71, 87, 101, 118, 136, 141; *Macbeth*, 10–11, 16, 34–36, 71, 109–10, 126 n.27; *Much Ado About Nothing*, 64–65, 92; *1 Henry IV*, 82; *Othello*, 19, 22, 82; *Richard III*, 9, 34–35, 65, 81, 85, 91, 98–99; *Romeo and Juliet*, 65; *The Winter's Tale* (adapted as *Florizel and Perdita*), 65
Sherbo, Arthur, 40, 45, 48
Sheridan, Richard Brinsley, 49, 144; as author of *The Rivals*, 46; author of *The School for Scandal*, 46
Sheridan, Thomas, 107, 120
She Stoops to Conquer (Goldsmith), 37, 45
Shirley, James, as author of *The Gamester*, 66
"The Sick Monkey" (Garrick), 97, 108–9
Siddons, Sarah, 128
society: eighteenth-century, 16, 22–23, 53, 65, 68, 88, 96, 110–18, 135–37, 140–50; Restoration, 12–13, 16–17, 19, 21, 128, 142–45
Southerne, Thomas, 62, 64; as author of *Oroonoko*, 98
Spencer, John, first earl of, 108

Spencer, Lady Georgiana, countess, 107–8
Stanislavsky, Constantin, 13, 149
Steele, Joshua, 57n
Steele, Richard, 34, 62, 67, 142, 144, 151–52 n.30
Stein, Elizabeth, 169
Sterne, Laurence, 46
Stockdale, Percival, 87
Stone, George Winchester, Jr., 3, 160–64, 166
Stone, Lawrence, 88, 169
Sturz, Helfrich Peter, 51
The Suspicious Husband (Benjamin Hoadly), 112
"sympathy," 89–90, 145–46; in an actor, 118–20, 127–28; in an audience, 118, 141–42, 146; as means of conceiving dramatic character, 34–36, 118–20, 133

The Theatrical Review, 164

Valborg, Henry Misson de, 31–32
Vanbrugh, John: as author of *The Provoked Husband* (with Colley Cibber), 64, 66–67; as author of *The Provoked Wife*, 68–69
Victor, Benjamin, 79–80
Voltaire (François-Marie Arouet), 64

Walmesley, Gilbert, 83–84, 112
Walpole, Horace, 18–22, 78–79, 111–12, 116–17, 120, 147, 163
The West Indian (Cumberland), 37–38
Whitehead, William: as author of *The Roman Father*, 48–49; as author of *The School for Lovers*, 37–38, 118
Wilkes, Thomas, 35
Wilkinson, Tate, 94, 163

About the Author

LEIGH WOODS is Assistant Professor of Theatre and Drama at Indiana University and has contributed articles to journals including *Shakespeare Quarterly* and *Themes in Drama*.